Poets
and
Prophets
of
Israel

CHURCH TRAINING COURSE 204

Prepared under the
auspices of the Church of God
General Department of Youth and
Christian Education

Poets and Prophets of Israel

Charles W. Conn

PATHWAY PRESS, Cleveland, Tennessee

Library of Congress Catalog Card Number: 80-84941

International Standard Book Number
cloth: 0-87148-707-1
paper: 0-87148-708-X

Copyright 1981
Pathway Press
Cleveland, Tennessee 37311

Printed in the United States of America

THE CHURCH TRAINING COURSE SERIES

Poets and Prophets of Israel, by Charles W. Conn, has been designated in the Church Training Course program as CTC 204. The Certificate of Credit (CTC 204c) will be awarded on the basis of the following requirements:

1. The written review and instructions for preparing the review are listed on page 131. The written review must be completed and reviewed by the pastor or someone he designates. Then the name of the student must be sent to the state office. (No grade will be given for the written review.)

2. The book must be read through.

3. Training sessions must be attended unless permission for absence is granted by the instructor.

4. The written review is not an examination. It is an overview of the text designed to reinforce the study. Students should search the text for the proper answers.

5. If no classes are conducted in this course of study, Church Training Course credit may be secured by home study.

A training record should be kept in the local church for each person who studies this and other courses in the Church Training Course program. A record form (CTC 33) will be furnished upon request from the state office.

TABLE OF CONTENTS

FOREWORD

The Bible is indeed the inspired Word of God. It is, as well, literature of much beauty and merit. Its pages account both with pathos and sublimity the history of a people and their relationship to their God. Though centuries old, its words still sear men's hearts and enlighten men's lives.

One-third of the entire Old Testament is poetry. This fact is obscured in those versions of Scripture which do not retain the poetic form but use strictly paragraph form. In this final book in his series of books on the Bible, Dr. Conn introduces the reader to the poetry of the Hebrew people. He explains the various forms of poetry found in Scripture and their uses.

A significant portion of Scripture is prophetical. Not all of Israel's prophets wrote, but those who did left us with material enough for many years of study. An almost endless volume of books have been published on this portion of Scripture. In a necessarily brief work, not much more than a glance at either the poets or the prophets of Israel and their writings could be accomplished. Dr. Conn, however, does a masterful job of gleaning the highlights and making real the happenings of Israel's history and the men and women who with God's guidance helped to shape that history.

Being a student of the Word, a lover of poetry, and one who appreciates skillful writing, I read with much enjoyment the rough draft of Charles W. Conn's *Poets and Prophets of Israel.* His love for the Word and appreciation of its beauty as great literature as well as the inspired Word of God shows forth clearly. His writing style is personal and congenial, as is the man,

and he leads the reader into a better understanding of
the technical aspects of Israel's poetry and of the times
in which the poets and prophets of Israel wrote. He
introduces the reader to some of the men who were
spiritual leaders of Israel and leaves one with not only
a greater knowledge of these men but also with a
greater understanding of them.

R. Lamar Vest
General Director
General Department of Youth
and Christian Education

PREFACE

Poets and Prophets of Israel is the seventh and final volume of the Christian Training Course series on the Bible. The first was completed nineteen years ago, October 9, 1961, and others have followed periodically since that time. Writing the biblical survey has been a pleasant task, and in many ways I am sorry it is over. A generation has passed during the preparation of the series; it is hoped that this generation will be as responsive to the final volume as the previous generation was to the first.

In several ways this volume has been the most enjoyable of the entire series. For one reason, I love poetry and it has been enjoyable to present the beauties of biblical poetry to students of our time. For another, it is gratifying to see the completion of the extended project. Finally, the wide acceptance of earlier studies gives some indication of what to anticipate about this crowning study.

I have worked with an excellent body of national youth and Christian education directors in the course of preparing the series. These men—Cecil B. Knight, Donald S. Aultman, Paul F. Henson, Cecil R. Guiles, Floyd D. Carey, Jr., R. Lamar Vest and Special Consultant Martin J. Baldree—have offered ready assistance but no intrusions of any kind.

Most of all, I appreciate my beloved Edna who, like the Muse of long ago, is my constant inspiration.

Now, regarding this present volume, I am especially grateful to my daughter, Mrs. Camilla Warren, who has carried the full load of manuscript preparation; her assistance has been invaluable. Later scriptural emendations were made by Mrs. Evaline Echols, my administrative assistant. Lamar Vest, the present youth and Christian education director, has been patient and wise in knowing when to nudge the project along.

Many books and various editions of the Bible have been helpful in the preparation of this study. I have followed the King James Version for the greater part, using those editions where the poetic sections are arranged in verse form. Unless otherwise noted, all quotations are from the King James Version. In several instances (five, to be exact) I have quoted from the Revised Standard Version, because of contemporary language that clarifies the archaisms of the older translation. I have also made constant reference to other versions not mentioned in the text. The Bibles and books that have been of particular benefit are:

Bibles

Chamberlin, Roy B. and Herman Feldman (eds.). *The Dartmouth Bible:* King James Version. Boston: Houghton Mifflin Company, 1950.

Lindsell, Harold (ed.). *Harper Study Bible:* Revised Standard Version. Grand Rapids, MI: Zondervan Publishing House, 1952.

The New English Bible. Oxford: Oxford University Press, 1970.

The Westminster Study Edition of the Holy Bible: King James Version. Philadelphia: The Westminster Press, 1948.

Books

Bullock, C. Hassell. *An Introduction to the Old Testament Poetic Books.* Chicago: Moody Press, 1979.

Freeman, Hobart E. *An Introduction to the Old Testament Prophets.* Chicago: Moody Press, 1968.

Goodspeed, Edgar J. *How to Read the Bible*. Philadelphia: Universal Book and Bible House, 1946.

Raven, John Howard. *Old Testament Introduction*. Old Tappan, NJ: Fleming H. Revell Company, 1910.

Robinson, George L. *The Twelve Minor Prophets*. Grand Rapids, MI: Baker Book House, 1952.

Unger, Merrill F. *Introductory Guide to the Old Testament*. Grand Rapids, MI: Zondervan Publishing House, 1951.

Charles W. Conn

Cleveland, Tennessee
October 9, 1980

The Poetry 1
of a People

From their beginning, the Israelites were a poetic people, expressing their deepest feelings in poetry and music. They used lofty phrases and elegant rhythms to express their depth of soul and breadth of life. Even before the Israelites were a distinct people, their early forefathers enriched the language with flights of poetic imagination and soulful declamations.

The Jews wrote poetry and sang songs from their dawn as a people to their demise as a nation. In their nomadic tents on the Judean tablelands, they sang of their troubles and trials, their conflicts and victories, their joys and sorrows, their labors and loves, and—most of all—their unshakable faith in God. Poetry was in the soul of the people.

WHAT IS POETRY?

Since poetry comprises one third of the entire Old Testament, it becomes helpful to our understanding if we know what poetry really is. It is elementary and erroneous to believe that it consists of nothing more than making the last words of parallel lines rhyme. Much of the greatest poetry has no rhyme at all.

Poetry is that art which uses words as both speech and song to express what the emotions feel, what the mind perceives and what the eye beholds. It is a measured mode of expression that makes use of imagination and rhythm to imprint itself upon the hearer's mind. It is chiefly distinguished by the feeling that inspires it and which it endeavors to communicate. Poetry, by its rhythmic and rhetorical language, integrates, intensifies and enhances the emotion it expresses.

English poetry uses rhythmic meter, alliteration, rhyme, stanzas and other devices to give the message of the poem drive and euphonious flow. When read or heard, it seems to soar in structured cadences. Prose, however well written, cannot sustain the imaginative power of poetry without resorting to certain poetic characteristics. In *How to Read the Bible*, Edgar J. Goodspeed says:

Poetry makes an imaginative demand upon the reader; he must yield to the poet's spell and follow him into the realm of imagination. To refuse to do this, and to treat the poet's flights as matter-of-fact statements would be disastrous in the extreme. . . So few versions of the English Bible distinguish its poetry from its prose that the reader must be on guard against mistaking one for the other, and treating it all as prose. For one thing, poetry is much more charged with emotion and excitement than prose; it is in general far more intense and filled with feeling.

HEBREW POETRY

Goodspeed states that *more than one third of the Old Testament is poetry.* Even the early sections of Genesis are interspersed with portions of poetry that antedate the Hebrew people. Unfortunately, the presence of poetry was largely overlooked until about two centuries ago. For instance, because the King James Version puts poetry in the same paragraph style used for prose, we tend to overlook the poetic beauty. Later translations do retain the poetic construction used in the original manuscripts; even some modern editions of the King James Version have restored the poetic form.

One of the earliest snatches of poetry we see is the "sword-song" of Lamech after he had killed a man. In the original text and in later translations Lamech's words are in their poetic form:

> Adah and Zillah, Hear my voice;
>   ye wives of Lamech, hearken unto my speech:
> for I have slain a man to my wounding
>   and a young man to my hurt.
> If Cain shall be avenged sevenfold,
>   truly Lamech seventy and sevenfold.
>
> *(Genesis 4:23, 24)*

PARALLELISM

Not only is Lamech's song one of the earliest uses of poetry in the Scriptures, but it is also an excellent example of *parallelism,* the primary style of Hebrew poetry. In this construction, there is no rhyme, no structured meter, no alliteration or other device associated with Western poetry; the poetry is found in the relationship of adjoining (or parallel) lines. There are various forms of parallelism, but the simplest and most easily recognized is *synonymous parallelism,* where the second line repeats, in different words, the same sentiment found in the first; the fourth line repeats, similarly, what is stated in the third, and so on. For example:

> Adah and Zillah // Hear my voice
>   *[is paralleled by]*
> ye wives of Lamech // hearken unto my speech;
> For I have slain a man to my wounding

> *[is paralleled by]*
> and a young man to my hurt.

> If Cain shall be avenged sevenfold
> *[is paralleled by]*
> truly Lamech seventy and sevenfold.

There is also *antithetic parallelism,* in which parallel lines express opposite or contrasting thoughts. Or two lines can be said to state positive and negative views of the same thought, as in the following:

> For the Lord knoweth the way of the righteous:
> but the way of the ungodly shall perish.
> *(Psalm 1:6)*

> In whose eyes a vile person is contemned;
> but he honoureth them that fear the Lord.
> *(Psalm 15:4)*

> The fear of the Lord prolongeth days:
> but the years of the wicked shall be shortened.
> *(Proverbs 10:27)*

Probably the most striking example of *antithetic parallelism* is found in Ecclesiastes 3:1-8:

> To every thing there is a season,
> and a time to every purpose under the heaven:
> A time to be born,
> and a time to die;
> A time to plant,
> and a time to pluck up that which is planted;

> A time to kill,
> and a time to heal;
> A time to break down,
> and a time to build up;

> A time to weep,
> and a time to laugh;
> A time to mourn,
> and a time to dance;

> A time to cast away stones,
>   and a time to gather stones together;
> A time to embrace,
>   and a time to refrain from embracing;
>
> A time to get,
>   and a time to lose;
> A time to keep,
>   and a time to cast away;
>
> A time to rend,
>   and a time to sew;
> A time to keep silence,
>   and a time to speak;
>
> A time to love,
>   and a time to hate;
> A time of war,
>   and a time of peace.

A third and considerably more emotional form is called *synthetic parallelism*, in which series of parallelisms occur in one poetic section, each line adding to and building upon the previous line. A beautiful example of this is found in the soaring repetitions of Psalm 103:

> Bless the Lord, O my soul:
>   and all that is within me, bless his holy name.
> Bless the Lord, O my soul,
>   and forget not all his benefits:
>   Who forgiveth all thine iniquities;
>   Who healeth all thy diseases;
>   Who redeemeth thy life from destruction;
>   Who crowneth thee with lovingkindness and
>   tender mercies;
>   Who satisfieth thy mouth with good things;
>   so that thy youth is renewed like the eagle's.

There are other, more complex, forms of parallelism in the poetry of the Bible, but it is not necessary to pursue them extensively here; there are excellent treatments of the subject available for those who wish to study the poetic structure more thoroughly.

PREVALENCE OF POETRY

The Hebrew Scriptures (the Old Testament) are saturated with poetry. Almost all the books contain poetic portions, and several consist totally of poetry. In Genesis, there are no fewer than eleven poems, ranging from the long oration of Jacob to his sons in Genesis 49:2-27, down to God's revelation to Rebekah concerning Jacob and Esau in Genesis 25:23:

> Two nations are in thy womb,
>> and two manner of people shall be separated from thy bowels;
>> and the one people shall be stronger than the other people;
>> and the elder shall serve the younger.

With the exception of six books—Leviticus, Ruth, 2 Kings, Nehemiah, Esther and Haggai—every book of the Old Testament has intermittent poetry in it. There are fifty poems in the Pentateuch and Historical Books, where one would least expect to find poetry. Among the most notable of these is the Song of Moses after the crossing of the Red Sea (Exodus 15:1-18), a long poem followed immediately by a shorter response by Miriam, who, with timbrels and dances, sang:

> Sing ye to the Lord, for he hath
>> triumphed gloriously;
> the horse and his rider hath he
>> thrown into the sea.

(Exodus 15:21)

This lovely poem of Miriam is the oldest hymn to

God found in Scripture. Such poetic outpourings
seem to have been spontaneous lyrics, improvised at
the time of some great event such as the crossing of
the sea.

Another such poem is Joshua's victory shout to the
sun and moon during a battle at Gibeon:

> Sun, stand thou still upon Gibeon;
>   and thou, Moon, in the valley of Ajalon.
> And the sun stood still, and the moon stayed,
>   until the people had avenged themselves upon
>   their enemies.
>
> *(Joshua 10:12, 13)*

Still another instance of poetic spontaneity is Samson's
exultant cry following his victory over the Philistines:

> With the jawbone of an ass, heaps upon heaps,
>   with the jaw of an ass have I slain a thousand men.
>
> *(Judges 15:16)*

The spontaneous lyrics of the women of Judah
following David's victory over Goliath, swept the kingdom and created a deep schism between David and
Saul:

> Saul hath slain his thousands,
>   and David his ten thousands.
>
> *(1 Samuel 18:7)*

SONGS OF THE EARTH

The Hebrews made poetry a part of their written
literature very early in their history and used it to
express almost every aspect of their lives: times of joy,
physical labor, parental anguish and blessing, and
laments at the death of friends. Nothing shows the
workaday use of poetry better than the song sung by

the Hebrews at the opening of a well near the border
of Moab:

> Spring up, O well; sing ye unto it:
> The princes digged the well,
> The nobles of the people digged it,
> By the direction of the lawgiver,
>   with their staves. . . .
>
> *(Numbers 21:17, 18)*

Among the laments in Hebrew poetry are David's
lament over Abner (2 Samuel 3:33, 34) and his beautiful utterance of soul at the death of Saul and Jonathan.
This poem is regarded as one of the two poetic
masterpieces in the Bible (the other being the Song of
Deborah in Judges 5). David's lament was carefully
prepared and shows the sensitive skill of the great
psalmist:

> The beauty of Israel is slain upon thy high places:
>   how are the mighty fallen!
>
> Tell it not in Gath,
>   publish it not in the streets of Askelon;
> lest the daughters of the Philistines rejoice,
>   lest the daughters of the uncircumcised triumph.
>
> Ye mountains of Gilboa, let there be no dew,
>   neither let there be rain, upon you, nor fields
>   of offerings:
> for there the shield of the mighty is vilely cast
>   away,
>   the shield of Saul, as though he had not been
>   anointed with oil.
>
> From the blood of the slain,
>   from the fat of the mighty,
> the bow of Jonathan turned not back,
>   and the sword of Saul returned not empty.
>
> Saul and Jonathan were lovely and pleasant in
>   their lives,
>   and in their death they were not divided:
> they were swifter than eagles,

they were stronger than lions.

Ye daughters of Israel, weep over Saul,
    who clothed you in scarlet, with other delights;
    who put on ornaments of gold upon your apparel.
How are the mighty fallen in the midst of the battle!
    O Jonathan, thou wast slain in thine high places.

I am distressed for thee, my brother Jonathan:
    very pleasant hast thou been unto me:
thy love to me was wonderful,
    passing the love of women.
How are the mighty fallen,
    and the weapons of war perished!

(2 Samuel 1:19-27)

Another poem of extraordinary power is the War Song of Deborah; it is one of the longest in the Bible—and one of the most beautiful. It deserves to be read in a version of the Bible that presents it in its poetic form. The epic poem consists of twelve scenes, built around the twelve tribes of Israel, all rich in imagination and atmosphere, that portray in vivid language the conditions of Israel at the time.

In the days of Shamgar the son of Anath,
In the days of Jael, the highways were unoccupied,
And the travellers walked through byways.
The inhabitants of the villages ceased,
    they ceased in Israel,
Until that I Deborah arose, that I arose
    a mother in Israel.

They chose new gods;
Then was war in the gates:
Was there a shield or spear seen
Among forty thousand in Israel?

*(Judges 5:6-8; the entire
poem covers verses 2-31)*

THE HISTORICAL POETRY

The following poems are interspersed through the Pentateuch and Historical Books; some are brief extracts and some are of considerable length. (The titles are obviously mine, drawn from the Scriptures where possible, and given merely for identification of the poems.)

Adam speaks of Eve	Genesis	2:23
God's judgment in Eden		3:14-17
Lamech's sword-speech		4:23, 24
Noah's curse of Canaan		9:25-27
Melchizedek blesses Abram		14:19, 20
God speaks to Rebekah		25:23
Isaac blesses Jacob		27:27-29
Isaac blesses Esau		27:39, 40
Jacob blesses Joseph's sons		48:15, 16
Jacob's added blessing		48:21
Jacob's patriarchal prophecy		49:2-27
The song of Moses	Exodus	15:1-18
Song of Miriam		15:21
Israel's benediction	Numbers	6:24-26
Song of the Well		21:14-18
Israel's victory at Heshbon		21:27-30
Prophetic discourses of Balaam		23:7-10
		23:18-24
		24:3-9
		24:15-24

Blessing and cursing of Israel	Deuteronomy	27:15-26
		28:3-6
		28:16-19
The song of Moses		32:1-43
Moses blesses Israel		33:2-29
Joshua's victory shout	Joshua	10:12, 13
The song of Deborah	Judges	5:2-31
Samson's riddle		14:14, 18
Samson on ass's jawbone		15:16
Prayer of Hannah	1 Samuel	2:1-10
Samuel speaks of obedience		15:22, 23
Women's song about David		18:7
		21:11
		29:5
David's lament over Jonathan	2 Samuel	1:19-27
David's lament over Abner		3:33, 34
Revolt of Sheba		20:1
David's song of deliverance		22:2-52
Last words of David		23:1-7
Solomon at Temple dedication	1 Kings	8:12, 13
Revolt of Israel		12:16
Amasai's pledge to David	1 Chronicles	12:18
Asaph's psalm of thanksgiving		16:8-36

Solomon at Temple dedication	2 Chronicles	5:13
		6:1, 2
Prayer of Solomon at dedication		6:41, 42
Praise of Israel at dedication		7:3
Revolt of Israel		10:16
Jehoshaphat's song of praise		20:21
Dedication of the second temple	Ezra	3:11

QUOTATIONS AND COLLECTIONS

Some of the poetry in the Old Testament is quoted from books not included in the canonical Scriptures. Joshua's dramatic order to the sun and moon is quoted from the *Book of Jasher* (Joshua 10:12, 13) as is David's lament over his dead friend Jonathan (2 Samuel 1:18).

The Song of the Well (Numbers 21:14) is quoted from the *Book of the Wars of the Lord*. Neither *Jasher* nor the *Book of Wars* is identified further, but it is commonly believed that they were anthologies or collections of Hebrew poetry.

The only poetic anthologies that have survived are what we call the Poetical Books—especially the Psalms.

THE POETIC BOOKS

Six books of the Bible are known as the Poetic Books because they consist entirely of poetry. These are:

JOB
PSALMS
PROVERBS
ECCLESIASTES
SONG OF SOLOMON
LAMENTATIONS

Because these books, which conspicuously and beau-
tifully reveal the language and techniques of poetry,
are indeed poetry, the question arises—are they accurate and inspired books? The answer is *yes*. God can
inspire poetry as well as prose. The language may be
more picturesque, the rhetoric more lofty, the imagery
more dramatic, but the declared truth and the recorded
facts are no less accurate. There is much figurative
speech in biblical poetry, but this is easily recognized
as such, and the truth expressed is not confused.

> There is a fire gone out of Heshbon.
>> *(Numbers 21:28)*
> Underneath are the everlasting arms.
>> *(Deuteronomy 33:27)*
> He hath also taken me by my neck,
>   and shaken me to pieces.
>> *(Job 16:12)*
> I am escaped with the skin of my teeth.
>> *(Job 19:20)*
> The pastures are clothed with flocks;
>   the valleys also are covered over with corn;
>   they shout for joy, they also sing.
>> *(Psalm 65:13)*
> Thou hast laid me in the lowest pit,
>   in darkness, in the deeps.
>> *(Psalm 88:6)*
> He shall cover thee with his feathers,
>   and under his wings shalt thou trust.
>> *(Psalm 91:4)*
> Let the floods clap their hands. . . .
>> *(Psalm 98:8)*

The beautiful, lyric language of poetry is actually an effective way to express the realities of God, for in poetry the imagination—and faith!—of man can soar.

POETRY IN THE PROPHETIC BOOKS

Among the sixteen Prophetic Books of the Old Testament, only the book of Haggai is totally in prose. On the other hand, there are six—Amos, Obadiah, Micah, Nahum, Habakkuk and Zephaniah—that are totally poetry. Another five—Isaiah, Jeremiah, Hosea, Joel and Malachi—are almost totally so. Only Haggai is altogether in prose. The prophets (which are dealt with in later chapters) found the poetic medium especially effective in their roles as God's spokesmen to His people, as interpreters of His Law and will to the people of Israel.

For the closing of this section, it seems appropriate to note the short gemlike Benediction of Israel, the beautiful blessing Aaron and his sons pronounced upon the people as they neared their promised land:

> The Lord bless thee, and keep thee:
> The Lord make his face shine upon thee,
>   and be gracious unto thee;
> The Lord lift up his countenance upon thee,
>   and give thee peace.
>
> *(Numbers 6:24-26)*

DISCUSSION QUESTIONS

1. More than one third of the Old Testament is written as poetry. Why do you think the poetic style is so effectively used in Scripture?

2. The primary style of Hebrew poetry is parallelism. Explain the use of this term. Name some of the various forms of parallelism and give an example of each.

3. Name the six books of the Bible known as the Poetic Books. Why are they so called? To what do they owe their particular beauty?

4. What are some of the ways the Psalms have affected your life personally? Give some examples.

5. What is the oldest hymn to God found in Scripture? By whom and on what occasion was it written?

Lyric Poetry   2

A large portion, fully one third, of the Hebrew Scriptures is in the form of poetry. Not all of the poetry is alike, for its writing covered a great span of time and the poems themselves represent many periods and styles of writing. The most apparent and popular poetic style in any age is *lyrical*, that which can be sung. Because of its melodic simplicity in form, its emotional strength in content, lyric poetry yields itself to the most common and popular usage.

The word *lyric* stems from *lyre*, a stringed instrument played usually as an accompaniment to singing. Popular songs, ballads, folk songs, and hymns are all lyrical in style and content. Most of the poetry in the Bible is lyrical, for much of it originated in spontaneous singing or was composed to be sung.

THE PSALMS

The largest collection of songs in the Bible is known to us as the Book of Psalms, which is very likely the most popular, most widely quoted, best-known book in the world. The 150 psalms in the collection are not only the finest religious lyrics of ancient Israel, but they rank among the immortal poetry of the world.

What we call the Book of Psalms was known by the ancients as the Psalter, from the word *psalterion*, which, like a lyre, was a stringed, harp-like instrument used to accompany singing. Sacred songs chanted or sung therefore came to be called psalms. It is important for us to bear in mind that the poetry in Psalms, exalted literature that it is, was created to be sung, not simply to be read. Indeed, the ancient Israelites probably knew the individual psalms only by singing, since written texts were available only to rulers, rabbis and scholars.

Singing of Psalms

The Book of Psalms consists of sacred songs collected over many years, written by many people and in many circumstances. The individual psalms were used for such purposes as divine worship, Temple ceremonies, national holy days, pilgrimage travel and private communion with God. As pilgrims marched up Mount Zion to the Temple, they chanted psalms as they ascended; on joyous days of celebration they united in the triumphant singing of appropriate psalms.

In New Testament days, the singing of psalms was part of sacred observance. Jesus and His disciples sang a psalm, or hymn, on His last night with them (Matthew 26:30). When He was crucified, He quoted from Psalm 22:1, "My God, my God, why hast thou forsaken me?" (Mark 15:34). Paul taught the Christians in Ephesus to encourage one another "in psalms and hymns and spiritual songs, singing and making melody in your heart to the Lord" (Ephesians 5:19).

Luke quotes Jesus as having referred to the Psalms in a doctrinal discussion (Luke 20:42). Peter in the Upper Room before Pentecost, also quoted the Book of Psalms as a prophetic and doctrinal source (Acts 1:20). This proves two things: First, the truths of Psalms are inspired Scripture, dependable sources for spiritual understanding. Second, the faith of the Lord is to be sung as well as preached. In his *Story of the Old Testament*, Edgar J. Goodspeed says:

Jewish religion expressed itself not only in laws and sermons but in hymns and prayers, and these were gathered up from time to time into collections, like our hymnbooks.

Martin Luther called Psalms "a Bible in miniature" because of the way it sings the truths of God into the human heart.

Who Wrote the Psalms?

As I said earlier, the Book of Psalms is the product of many hands and many hearts, which, like a good hymnbook, represents the creative genius and spiritual sensitivity of many souls. David is said to have written seventy-three psalms, almost half of the total. For this reason men usually speak of "the Psalms of David," as if he were author of all. But he was not, as we learn from the headnotes that from antiquity have been affixed to many of the individual psalms. From these inscriptions we find that twelve were composed by Asaph, eleven by the sons of Korah, two by Solomon, one by Moses, one by Heman the Ezrahite, one by Ethan the Ezrahite, and one by a person known simply as "one afflicted, when he is faint and pours out his complaint before the Lord" (Psalm 102).

There were also many circumstances that gave rise to particular psalms. Fifteen are called "Songs of Ascents" (or, "of Degrees" in the King James Version), which are believed to be those sung by worshipers as they ascended to the Temple on Mount Zion. Like any good hymnbook of the present, many psalms are inscribed to certain persons, such as David's dedication: "To the chief Musician, even to Jeduthum" (Psalm 39). Fifty-five of the psalms are inscribed to "the chief musician," sometimes but not always named. These are accompanied by what appear to be technical instructions to the musicians. We cannot with certainty decipher such directions as, "To the chief Musician on Neginoth upon Sheminith" (Psalm 6). We are also uncertain about the word *Selah* that appears in thirty-nine of the psalms, although some scholars believe it to be a suggestion to the singers to lift their voices. Others believe the word marks a vocal pause for an orchestral intermezzo. No one really knows.

The Five Divisions

From antiquity, the Psalms have been arranged in a fivefold division. The reason for this structure is not clear, but it seems to be done in an effort to make the Psalms correspond with the five books of the Torah, or Pentateuch. The divisions are as follows:

Book I	Psalms 1-41
Book II	Psalms 42-72
Book III	Psalms 73-89
Book IV	Psalms 90-106
Book V	Psalms 107-150

Each of the five sections closes with a doxology, a short hymn of praise to God, which helped determine the dividing point of the five sections. They are as follows:

Blessed be the Lord God of Israel,
  from everlasting, and to everlasting!
Amen, and Amen.

(Psalm 41:13)

Blessed be the Lord God, the God of Israel,
  who only doeth wondrous things.
And blessed be his glorious name forever:
  and let the whole earth be filled with his glory;
Amen, and Amen.

(Psalm 72:18, 19)

> Blessed be the Lord for evermore.
> Amen, and Amen.
>
> *(Psalm 89:52)*
>
> Blessed be the Lord God of Israel
> from everlasting to everlasting:
> And let all the people say, Amen.
> Praise ye the Lord!
>
> *(Psalm 106:48)*

The fifth division, and the entire Book of Psalms, then concludes with a series of doxologies, or what has been called the "Great Doxology":

> Praise ye the Lord, Praise God in his sanctuary:
> praise him in the firmament of his power.
> Praise him for his mighty acts:
> praise him according to his excellent greatness.
> Praise him with the sound of the trumpet:
> praise him with the psaltery and harp.
> Praise him with the timbrel and dance:
> praise him with stringed instruments and organs.
> Praise him upon the loud cymbals:
> praise him upon the high sounding cymbals.
> Let every thing that hath breath praise the Lord.
> Praise ye the Lord.
>
> *(Psalm 150)*

Whatever the original reason for dividing the Psalms into five divisions, it makes a convenient arrangement for study of the separate psalms. It is believed by some that the determining factor of the five books was the predominant manner in which the name of God is employed in each division. Whatever the basic reason, it, like many other peculiarities of the canonical structure, is now lost in antiquity.

Classification of the Psalms

Some of the 150 psalms were written spontaneously as statements of praise for particular blessings; others were written specifically for worship in the Temple; some are personal; some are congregational. Dr. C. Hassell Bullock, formerly of Lee College, in his *Introduction to the Old Testament Poetical Books*, cites seven types or classes of psalms as having been set forth by earlier scholars.

1. Hymns, sung on holy days at the Temple.
2. Community laments, chanted by the people when disaster had struck.
3. Songs of the individual, sung by pious persons.
4. Thank offering songs, sung by one who had been delivered from great distress, and accompanied by a thank offering.
5. Laments of the individual, intoned by one who had suffered physical or emotional affliction.
6. Entrance liturgies, chanted by those who desired to enter the place of worship.
7. Royal psalms, sung in honor of the king.

Dr. J. H. Eaton, in his *Torch Commentary on Psalms*, makes use of the same basal classifications, and then concludes: "valuable as such classification is . . . to determine the original use and meaning of particular psalms is still no simple matter."

In a similar way, many of our Christian hymns were written for a specific purpose and later adopted for more general purposes. For example, "Onward Christian Soldiers" was written as a children's march tune, but it has now become a standard song in general worship services.

Inspiration in Psalms

Aside from its literary beauty and historical interest, the Book of Psalms is both the product and the source of immense inspiration. Because the Psalms speak *from*

every human circumstance, they speak *to* every human
need. John Paterson, in his *Praises of Israel*, calls
Psalms "the peculiar possession of all God's children.
. . . Age after age turns to this refreshing fountain for
comfort and renewal and finds here 'a well of water
springing up to everlasting life.' "

The Psalms grew out of the experiences of a particular people, yet they speak the language of all people.
They grew in a land no larger than the State of
Vermont, yet they speak to, and answer, the spiritual
needs of all the world. For instance, the First Psalm,
its lyrical beauty equalled by its universal spiritual
insight, says:

> Blessed is the man that walketh not in the counsel
>   of the ungodly,
>   nor standeth in the way of sinners,
>   nor sitteth in the seat of the scornful.
> But his delight is in the law of the Lord;
>   and in his law doth he meditate day and night.
> And he shall be like a tree planted by the rivers
>   of water,
>   that bringeth forth his fruit in his season;
> his leaf also shall not wither;
>   and whatsoever he doeth shall prosper.
>
> The ungodly are not so:
>   but are like the chaff which the wind driveth
>   away.
> Therefore the ungodly shall not stand in the
>   judgment,
>   nor sinners in the congregation of the righteous.
> For the Lord knoweth the way of the righteous:
>   but the way of the ungodly shall perish.
>   *(Psalm 1:1-6)*

Or consider, what man who has felt the burden of
guilt and failure can fail to identify with David after
the great king of Israel had sinned?

Have mercy upon me, O God, according to thy
     lovingkindness:
  according unto the multitude of thy tender
     mercies blot out my transgressions.
Wash me throughly from mine iniquity,
  and cleanse me from my sin.

For I acknowledge my transgressions:
  and my sin is ever before me.
Against thee, thee only, have I sinned,
  and done this evil in thy sight:
that thou mightest be justified when thou speakest,
  and be clear when thou judgest.

Make me to hear joy and gladness;
  that the bones which thou hast broken may rejoice.
Hide thy face from my sins,
  and blot out all mine iniquities.

Create in me a clean heart, O God;
  and renew a right spirit within me.
Cast me not away from thy presence;
  and take not thy holy spirit from me.
Restore unto me the joy of thy salvation;
  and uphold me with thy free spirit.

(Psalm 51:1-4; 8-12)

Just as David's prayer for forgiveness came from a
personal failure, there are other expressions that reveal a more triumphant side of life. It was possibly
Moses who, in the Sinai wilderness, wrote Psalm 91,
with its great assurances of trust in God. We may
experience wildernesses of other kinds, but the truths
of God are the same:

He that dwelleth in the secret place of the most
     High
  shall abide under the shadow of the Almighty.
I will say of the Lord, He is my refuge and my
     fortress:
  my God; in him will I trust.

Surely he shall deliver thee from the snare of the
    fowler,
    and from the noisome pestilence.
He shall cover thee with his feathers,
    and under his wings shalt thou trust:
    his truth shall be thy shield and buckler.
Thou shalt not be afraid for the terror by night;
    nor for the arrow that flieth by day;
    Nor for the pestilence that walketh in darkness;
    nor for the destruction that wasteth at noonday.
A thousand shall fall at thy side,
    and ten thousand at thy right hand;
    but it shall not come nigh thee.
There shall no evil befall thee,
    neither shall any plague come nigh thy dwelling.
For he shall give his angels charge over thee,
    to keep thee in all thy ways.
They shall bear thee up in their hands,
    lest thou dash thy foot against a stone.

(Psalm 91:1-7; 10-12)

Or, who can match the despair of the psalmist in
Psalm 130, who said, "Out of the depths have I cried
unto thee, O Lord. Lord, hear my voice. . . ."

What lonely soul can fail to see the melancholy of
the Israelites when they were exiled in a foreign land
and separated from everything familiar and stable to
them? Their haunting song comes across the centuries
and the earth to us today.

By the rivers of Babylon, there we sat down,
    yea, we wept, when we remembered Zion.
    We hanged our harps upon the willows in the
        midst thereof.
For there they that carried us away captive
        required of us a song;
    and they that wasted us required of us mirth,
        saying,
    Sing us one of the songs of Zion.
How shall we sing the Lord's song in a strange land?

> If I forget thee, O Jerusalem,
>> let my right hand forget her cunning.
> If I do not remember thee,
>> let my tongue cleave to the roof of my mouth;
>> if I prefer not Jerusalem above my chief joy.
>
>>>> *(Psalm 137:1-6)*

One of the happiest Christian experiences is the steeping of oneself in the Psalms. (I keep at hand an edition that preserves both the poetic verse style and the familiar phrases of the King James Version, lest I lose any of the beauty and impact of the sublime songs.) There is treasure in every page, whatever our need or mood. The person fretting over financial straits can see himself in such confessions as:

> Truly God is good to Israel,
>> even to such as are of a clean heart.
> But as for me, my feet were almost gone;
>> my steps had well nigh slipped.
> For I was envious at the foolish,
>> when I saw the prosperity of the wicked.
>
> Behold, these are the ungodly, who prosper in the
>> world;
>> they increase in riches.
> When I thought to know this,
>> it was too painful for me;
>> Until I went into the sanctuary of God;
>> then understood I their end.
> Surely thou didst set them in slippery places:
>> thou castedst them down into destruction.
>
>>>> *(Psalm 73:1-3, 12,*
>>>> *16-18)*

Or, who does not recognize himself in this reminder not to envy the prosperity of evil men?

> Fret not thyself because of evildoers,
>> neither be thou envious against the workers
>> of iniquity.

For they shall soon be cut down like the grass,
  and wither as the green herb.

Trust in the Lord, and do good;
    so shalt thou dwell in the land, and verily
      thou shalt be fed.
Delight thyself also in the Lord;
    and he shall give thee the desires of thine
      heart.
Commit thy way unto the Lord;
    trust also in him; and he shall bring it to pass.

(Psalm 37:1-5)

Joyful Psalms

The Book of Psalms is essentially a book of joy, worship, praise and trust. We see pilgrims on their way to feasts in Jerusalem, singing:

I was glad when they said unto me,
  Let us go into the house of the Lord.

(Psalm 122:1)

then, changing to another psalm as they near Mount Zion:

Who shall ascend into the hill of the Lord?
  Or who shall stand in his holy place?

(Psalm 24:3)

and then, like an antiphony, the answer comes forth from the group:

He that hath clean hands, and a pure heart;
  who hath not lifted up his soul unto vanity,
  nor sworn deceitfully.

(Psalm 24:4)

And at last, inside the waiting gates of His sanctuary, the pilgrims sing together;

Make a joyful noise unto the Lord, all ye lands.
    Serve the Lord with gladness:
    come before his presence with singing.
Know ye that the Lord he is God:
    it is he that hath made us, and not we ourselves;
    we are his people, and the sheep of his pasture.
Enter into his gates with thanksgiving,
    and into his courts with praise:
    be thankful unto him, and bless his name.
For the Lord is good;
    his mercy is everlasting;
    and his truth endureth to all generations.
                       (Psalm 100)

But in Jerusalem or the countryside, the people of God were assured of His watchcare. Whether in Judea or faraway America many centuries later, the one psalm that speaks to every heart and every need is that which we call "The Shepherd Psalm," which is lovely as a pastoral hymn and exalted as a song of praise.

The Lord is my shepherd;
    I shall not want.
    He maketh me to lie down in green pastures:
    he leadeth me beside the still waters.
    He restoreth my soul:
    he leadeth me in the paths of righteousness
        for his name's sake.
Yea, though I walk through the valley of the shadow
        of death,
    I will fear no evil:
    for thou art with me;
    thy rod and thy staff they comfort me.
Thou preparest a table before me in the presence
        of mine enemies:
    thou anointest my head with oil;
    my cup runneth over.
Surely goodness and mercy shall follow me all the
        days of my life:
    and I will dwell in the house of the Lord for ever.
                        (Psalm 23)

DISCUSSION QUESTIONS

1. Most of the poetry in the Bible is lyrical in style. Explain this term.

2. By whom were the Psalms written? Explain some of the circumstances of their writing.

3. The Psalms are arranged into five sections. Name some points which seem to characterize these divisions.

4. Name seven types or classifications of the Psalms as they were written or sung by the people.

5. Though the Psalms began with a particular people in a small land, they still speak to the spiritual needs of all the world. To what do you attribute this fact?

Narrative Poetry

Narrative poetry is that which tells a story and follows a plot. Sometimes called dramatic poetry, it usually has a central character and is woven around a particular theme. But the greater part of Old Testament poetry is lyrical, philosophical or prophetic (which are considered in other chapters of this study). There are two poems, however, that are narrative, or dramatic, in nature: The Book of Job and The Song of Solomon.

These tell a story of sorts; they follow a general theme and develop central characters. Unlike action drama, however, these consist almost entirely of dialogue—songs and speeches—with very little action. It is almost as if they were written to be presented on a stage—which is why they are often referred to as drama.

JOB

The Book of Job, possibly the world's oldest drama, begins with two chapters of prose (chs. 1, 2) that introduce the theme of all the dialogue that follows; and concludes with an epilogue that explains how the drama of Job ends (42:7-17). Virtually everything in between is poetry—poetry so powerful that it is utterly captivating in verse form, and even manages to break through the paragraph arrangement of the King James Version.

Job is possibly the oldest book of the Bible and is also one of the earliest dramatic works of any literature. It is commonly believed to date back to the earliest Hebrew times, even as far back as the time of Abraham. Some scholars disagree with such antiquity and date it much later. That is only one of many things we do not know about the book. For instance, we have no precise knowledge about the land of Uz, where Job lived, for it is not mentioned in any other book of the Bible. Although some scholars suggest that it was a region near Edom, all efforts to verify its location have failed. Where Uz was, we can only speculate about today.

Neither is there evidence that Job was a Hebrew at all. Some people assume that he was, but it is just that—an assumption. Nothing in the book proves it. *The Dartmouth Bible* says: "Indeed, so much is left to the imagination that the book appears to have been designed to escape the limitations of time or place."

The Theme

The central theme of the book can best be stated in the question: Why do good men suffer? Job was a righteous man who suffered much. In the beginning, God vouches for His servant's goodness, when He says to Satan: "Hast thou considered my servant Job, that there is none like him in the earth, a perfect and an upright man, one that feareth God, and escheweth evil?" (1:8).

Yet Job suffered in virtually every human way: loss of wealth, loss of family, loss of respect, scorn by his wife, criticism by his friends, physical affliction; and, worst of all, his suffering was compounded by an unawareness of why calamity had befallen him. Every person who suffers and wonders why can look back to the inexplicable battering Job took and find strength to endure.

In him we see inner strength triumph over outward circumstances. The issues of pain and confusion are detailed with such graphic intensity that the reader finds himself being drawn into Job's search for reason and assurance. In reading the story of Job, one becomes impatient toward prejudice, indignant at hypocrisy, and delighted when truth is vindicated at last. That is drama at its very best.

The Person

The obvious question that arises is whether or not Job was an actual person. Did such a person really live, or is Job an imaginary character in a piece of dramatic fiction? Fortunately, we do not have to ponder the question long, for the answer is easily found. Job was an actual person who experienced the events described in the book; we know this because he is twice mentioned as a historical person in other books of the Bible.

Ezekiel 14:20 mentions Job along with Noah and Daniel as an example of righteousness. In the New Testament, James refers to his patience in suffering:

> Behold, we count them happy which endure. Ye have heard of the patience of Job, and have seen the end of the Lord; that the Lord is very pitiful and of tender mercy.
>
> *(James 5:11)*

Job was certainly real enough, which is why he speaks so clearly to men of all ages. His frustrations, confusion, honesty, even his occasional complaints and lapses into self-pity stamp him as being intensely human. He comes through to us as a person determined to maintain his moral integrity under whatever hurts might come to him. Only a man of great character could take the worst that Satan could do to him and still rejoice in the good that God would do for him.

Job became a testing ground between God and Satan. He suffered not because he had sinned, but because God knew he would not sin.

The Story of Job

The story of Job is introduced in the first two chapters of the book, which constitute a prologue for the drama that follows. Job was a man of wealth and influence in a place called Uz, a man whose piety equalled his favored circumstances. He became a target of Satan, who arrogantly suggested to the Lord that all the earth belonged to him rather than to God (1:7, 2:2). God rejected this claim of Satan and cited to him the steadfast devotion of Job.

Satan scoffed at the mention of Job's name and accused him of pretending to love God for the benefits he received from Him. God's confidence in Job and Satan's contempt for him made him a proving point for the two points of view. In order that Satan's blasphemy against God and man be eternally denounced and proved a lie, God allowed Satan to test Job, to assail his devotion to God, even to take away the benefits for which Satan claimed that Job served God.

In rapid succession, the devil snatched every benefit away: possessions, honor and family, so that nothing but his love for God remained. Bereft of every blessing, Job said to his wife:

> Naked came I out of my mother's womb,
>   and naked shall I return thither:
> the Lord gave, and the Lord hath taken away;
>   blessed be the name of the Lord.
>
> *(Job 1:21)*

When Satan's scheme failed, the Wicked One accused Job a second time, by suggesting that physical affliction would prove the shallowness of Job's devotion to God (2:4, 5). God's confidence in His servant was so great that He permitted that point to be tested, and Job was subjected to a plague of painful boils. At that point, even Job's wife scorned him and suggested that he abandon his integrity, curse God and die (2:9). With his rejection by his wife, Job was stripped of every earthly support that undergirded him. He stood alone, with nothing but his inner resources to sustain him.

Thereupon, three friends, hearing of Job's unprecedented calamities, came to Uz to console and comfort him. These friends contemplated with Job the reason why he was subjected to such pain and loss.

The Discourses

Following the two prose chapters, which give the background I have related, the rest of the Book of Job consists of dialogues between Job and his three friends—Bildad, Eliphaz and Zophar. All three give long discourses on what they think has happened to Job, and Job gives a long response to each discourse. The discourses, which occupy chapters 3:1-42:6, are given in poetic form—and it is poetry of the highest sort.

(The Book of Job deserves to be read frequently for its beauty alone—but in an edition that preserves the poetic form. Its depth of wisdom and its story of devotion make it a rich spiritual experience.)

Job begins the discourses with his friends, with words that immediately reveal his depth of sorrow and weariness of life:

> Let the day perish wherein I was born,
>> and the night in which it was said, There is
>> a man child conceived.
> Let that day be darkness;
>> let not God regard it from above,
>> neither let the light shine upon it.
> Let darkness and the shadow of death stain it;
>> let a cloud dwell upon it;
>> let the blackness of the day terrify it.
> Because it shut not up the doors of my mother's
>> womb,
>> nor hid sorrow from mine eyes.
>
> *(3:3-5, 10)*

Job would return to this emotion at other times as he discussed the unexpected and unexplained troubles that had befallen him.

> My soul is weary of my life;
>> I will leave my complaint upon myself;
>> I will speak in the bitterness of my soul.
>
> *(10:1)*
>
> Wherefore then hast thou brought me forth out of
>> the womb?
>> Oh that I had given up the ghost, and no eye
>> had seen me!
>
> *(10:18)*

Each of the three friends, in the course of the dialogues, made three speeches, each with a response from Job. These are recorded in sequence:

The Discourses and Responses

ELIPHAZ	BILDAD	ZOPHAR
chs. 4-7	chs. 8-10	chs. 11-14
chs. 15-17	chs. 18-19	chs. 20-21
chs. 22-24	chs. 25-27:6	ch. 28

Presumptuous Friends

From the beginning, Job's friends presumed that his troubles were the result of some evil in his life. Their personal judgments had individual aspects, but all were essentially the same: The Lord had abandoned Job because he had sinned.

First, Eliphaz saw Job's suffering as a proof of his guilt, and smugly admonished him to seek the Lord:

> Even as I have seen, they that plow iniquity,
>   and sow wickedness, reap the same. . . .
> I would seek unto God,
>   and unto God would I commit my cause.
>   *(4:8; 5:8)*

To which Job bitterly responded that one who calls himself a friend should manifest pity:

> To him that is afflicted
>   pity should be shewed from his friends;
> But he forsaketh the fear of the Almighty.
> My brethren have dealt deceitfully as a brook,
>   and as the stream of brooks they pass away.
>   *(6:14, 15)*

Bildad added his reproach next, pointing out with equal smugness that God would not allow evil to befall any but evildoers:

> Behold, God will not cast away a perfect man,
> Neither will he help the evildoers.
>   *(8:20)*

Zophar spoke last, and added his self-righteous opinion that Job's suffering, great as it was, was less than he deserved:

> Know therefore that God exacteth of thee
> less than thine iniquity deserveth.
> *(11:6)*

To each of the discourses, Job responded with an assertion of his innocence and a search for understanding. The three speeches of each friend and Job's response to each speech, constitute the deepest spiritual insight and the loftiest literature in the Old Testament. Edgar J. Goodspeed, in *How to Read the Bible*, says:

> Was there ever such rhetoric as that in the Book of Job? It fairly overwhelms the reader like a huge wave. Its insight, its imagery, its wealth of symbols, its power of expansion, its depth of feeling sweep on in unabated flood through forty pages, unmatched in literature.

Job's Steadfastness

Twice more each of the friends spoke, and insisted upon the guilt of Job. But the steadfast faith of Job shines through his pain-filled responses like a beacon for all ages. Not knowing what was happening to him, even believing for a while that God had turned against him, Job still declared his faith:

> Hold your peace, let me alone, that I may speak,
> and let come on me what will.
> Wherefore do I take my flesh in my teeth,
> and put my life in mine hand?
> Though he slay me, yet will I trust in him:
> but I will maintain mine own ways before him.
> He also shall be my salvation:
> for a hypocrite shall not come before him.
> *(13:13-16)*

Not knowing but what he would die in such a state, Job declared such steadfast faith that even now we turn to it when speaking of immortality:

> For I know that my redeemer liveth,
>> and that he shall stand at the latter day upon
>> the earth:
> And though after my skin worms destroy this body,
>> yet in my flesh shall I see God:
> Whom I shall see for myself,
>> and mine eyes shall behold, and not another.
>> *(19:25-27)*

Final Vindication

A fourth man appeared on the scene late in the book, Elihu in chapters 32-37, but no one paid much attention to his rather pompous condemnation of Job.

In chapters 38-41, however, God intervened on behalf of His patient servant. The words of the Lord are a rare and beautiful declaration of His ways in the universe. He then rebuked Job for his rash inference that his human wisdom could ascertain and fathom the ways of God:

> Gird up thy loins now like a man:
>> I will demand of thee,
>> And declare thou unto me.
> Wilt thou also disannul my judgment?
>> Wilt thou condemn me, that thou mayest be
>> righteous?
> Hast thou an arm like God?
>> Or canst thou thunder with a voice like him?
>> *(40:7-9)*

It would be well today if those who presume always to know the will and ways of God, who claim no need to pray "Thy will be done," could understand this: His ways are higher than our ways and His thoughts are higher than our thoughts, as the heavens are higher than the earth (Isaiah 55:8, 9).

Upon hearing the words of the Lord, Job repented of his rashness and lack of understanding:

> I know that thou canst do every thing,
>   and that no thought can be withholden from thee.
> . . . therefore have I uttered that I understood not;
>   things too wonderful for me, which I knew not.
> I have heard of thee by the hearing of the ear:
>   but now mine eye seeth thee:
> Wherefore I abhor myself, and repent
>   in dust and ashes.

(42:2, 3, 5, 6)

Following Job's prayer, the Book of Job concludes with a brief prose epilogue (42:7-17), which relates how the patriarch was vindicated and how all that once was lost was restored to him. It is one of the most inspiring and insightful books of the Old Testament.

SONG OF SOLOMON

This narrative poem is a far cry from Job. There the mood was solemn and the subject contemplative; here the mood is happy and the subject is romantic love. Christian responses to the book have varied: Some are offended by a book of such frank and sensuous language; some are mystified by its subject of physical love; some are unable to accommodate the fact that it does not mention the name of God.

It is stated that it is the work of Solomon (1:1), so it must be concluded that it is more than poetry of love. The love of the bride and bridegroom must represent some deeper, more spiritual aspect of love. Once these matters are reconciled in the reader's mind, the exquisite poetry can be relished for both its beauty and its spiritual purpose. The book refers to the love of God (the bridegroom) and Israel (the bride), and to Christ (the bridegroom) and the Church (the bride). Several New Testament references indicate that this is a correct interpretation. (See Ephesians 5:22-29; Matthew 25:1-10; Revelation 21:9; 22:17.)

Read as Poetry

There is no reason to belabor the point of allegory, symbolism or undue interpretation. The Song of Solomon (or, Song of Songs, as it is called in chapter 1:1) is beautiful poetry, to be read with enjoyment and benefit as great literature. The spiritual interpretation should not become a weight that hinders the flow of lyricism or the flight of imagery. Every person who loves the Word of God should immerse himself in the beautiful book and not strain for precise interpretation. Let the book speak to you as it will.

It is a beautiful set of poems that describe the love of the King (Solomon) and his bride (a maiden referred to as the Shulamite in 6:13). The narrative plan has the maiden speaking to the king, and the king to the maiden, the maiden to the court women, and the women to the maiden. It is important that we know who is speaking to whom if we are to benefit most from our study of the Song. (Some Bibles have subheads that clarify this for us; such as *The Scofield Bible*, *The Dartmouth Bible*, *The Living Bible*, and various study editions of the Bible.)

The Story

The story told in the Song is lovely: The mighty king sees and loves a young maiden in his vineyards. She, who is dark from the sun and accustomed to hard labor, is delighted that one so splendid and mighty should notice her. In time, however, she becomes indifferent to his interest and begins to spurn his attention. He who has been attentive and concerned for her then withdraws and she is left alone. When she realizes what she has done, she becomes frantic and searches for her King. When she finds him again, he receives her readily and they are reunited with gladness of heart.

The story adapts well to Christ's relationship to the Church, which makes it a popular source of preaching and teaching. Nothing in the world of literature is more beautiful than "The Maiden's Soliloquy," as she awaits her beloved:

> The voice of my beloved!
>   behold, he cometh
>   leaping upon the mountains,
>   skipping upon the hills.
> My beloved is like a roe
>   or a young hart:
>   behold, he standeth
>   behind our wall,
>   he looketh forth at the windows,
>   showing himself through the lattice.
> My beloved spake, and said unto me,
>   Rise up, my love, my fair one,
>   and come away.
>   For, lo, the winter is past,
>   the rain is over and gone;
> The flowers appear on the earth;
>   the time of the singing
>   of birds is come,
>   and the voice of the turtle
>   is heard in our land:
> The fig tree putteth forth her green figs,
>   and the vines with the tender grape
>   give a good smell.

> Arise, my love, my fair one,
> and come away.
>
> *(2:8-13)*

As the love of the king and the maiden is secured in their communion of hearts, she makes a wonderful commitment to him, a pledge both wise and tender:

> Set me as a seal upon thine heart,
>   as a seal upon thine arm:
> for love is strong as death;
>   jealousy is cruel as the grave:
>   the coals thereof are coals of fire,
>   which hath a most vehement flame.
> Many waters cannot quench love,
>   neither can the floods drown it.
>
> *(8:6, 7)*

Every bride should feel so toward her husband, and he to her. The Church, likewise, should make that its commitment to Christ.

DISCUSSION QUESTIONS

1. The Book of Job and the Song of Solomon are classified as narrative or dramatic poetry. What are some of the characteristics that make them such?

2. What proof do we have that Job was an actual person who lived and not just an imaginary character?

3. Why do you think God allowed Satan to test Job so severely?

4. What common accusation did the three so-called friends voice against Job? Does this remind you of a similar error in our present day?

5. In the Song of Solomon what deeper spiritual meaning is set forth by the love of Solomon for his bride?

6. What is the greatest pleasure you derive from reading the Song of Solomon?

Wisdom Poetry

4

A prominent place was given to Wisdom Poetry in the Hebrew Bible. Like other ancient peoples, the Hebrews were fond of aphorisms, maxims, similes, parables and other pungent ways of communicating ideas. These modes of expression are most effective in pointed, terse poetry. So we see a sprinkling of such poetry throughout the Old Testament (as I have discussed in Chapter One). There are three complete books that follow the aphoristic style: Proverbs, Ecclesiastes and Lamentations.

The writing of maxims, called proverbs in the Bible, is a practical and effective way of communicating truth without long and ponderous philosophical treatises. It is still a popular way, but it requires much more skill than does conventional writing. Charles Spurgeon said that a proverb must have brevity, point—and salt! A maxim is a deft turn of a phrase that makes its truth stick in the hearer's mind.

The subjects of the brief, catchy statements in the Bible are usually practical rather than theoretical; they deal with human behavior, domestic affairs and other equally workaday matters. The Wisdom Literature of the Bible has been called "God stooping from heaven to chart for man a safe course through this world."

PROVERBS

The Book of Proverbs, like the Psalms, is a literary collection, not the work of only one man. It is customary to speak of "the Proverbs of Solomon" in the same way we speak of "the Psalms of David," but it is equally inaccurate. Proverbs is the creative product of at least four men, the chief of which is Solomon.

In 1 Kings 4:32 we read that Solomon "spake three thousand proverbs: and his songs were a thousand and five." In his comprehensive literary genius, "he spake of trees, from the cedar tree that is in Lebanon even unto the hyssop that springeth out of the wall: he spake also of beasts, and of fowl, and of creeping things, and of fishes" (1 Kings 4:33). His wisdom was of such renown that "there came of all people to hear the wisdom of Solomon, from all kings of the earth, which had heard of his wisdom" (1 Kings 4:34).

It has been aptly stated that what Moses was to Hebrew Law, and David was to Hebrew music, Solomon was to Hebrew wisdom. But all that remains of his prodigious literary output are portions of the Proverbs and Ecclesiastes, the Song of Songs and two psalms.

It is not easy to read the Proverbs. There is no plan or systematic arrangement to the approximately eight hundred proverbs in the book. They are excellent for browsing, picking out a witty saying here and there, but they do not yield to serious reading. The lack of continuity in the verses makes each proverb separate from the others, standing alone, and builds no sustained direction.

The proverbs do, however, fall into an arrangement of sorts, with a division by writers that can be observed. We can identify at least four writers and even more divisions.

Divisions of the Proverbs

The Proverbs fall into six natural divisions, each of which has an opening autograph that identifies the writer.

1. The Proverbs of Solomon, the son of David, king of Israel (chapters 1-9)
2. The Proverbs of Solomon (chapters 10-22:16)
3. The Words of the Wise (chapters 22:17-24:34)
4. Proverbs of Solomon, which the men of Hezekiah king of Judah copied out (chapters 25-29)
5. The Words of Agur the son of Jakeh, even the prophecy (chapter 30)
6. The Words of King Lemuel, the prophecy that his mother taught him (chapter 31)

First Section

The first section emphasizes the merits of wisdom, and contrasts wisdom with folly. The purposes of wisdom are stated in such parallelisms as:

> To give subtilty to the simple,
>   to the young man knowledge and discretion.
>   *(1:4)*

> The fear of the Lord is the beginning of knowledge:
>   but fools despise wisdom and instruction.
>   *(1:7)*

> When wisdom entereth into thine heart,
>   and knowledge is pleasant unto thy soul;
> Discretion shall preserve thee,
>   understanding shall keep thee. . . .
> Happy is the man that findeth wisdom
>   and the man that getteth understanding.
>   *(2:10, 11; 3:13)*

Wisdom is personified and spoken of in the feminine gender (I have added the italics for emphasis):

> *Her* ways are the ways of pleasantness. . . .
>   *(3:17)*
> *She* is a tree of life to them that lay hold upon *her*.
>   *(3:18)*
> Love *her*, and *she* shall keep thee. . . .
>   *(4:6)*
> *She* shall bring thee honour, when thou dost embrace *her*.
>
>   *(4:8)*
> Wisdom hath builded *her* house
>   *She* hath hewn out *her* seven pillars. . . .
>   *(9:1)*

By this personification, wisdom is exalted as friend, lover, companion, and all other relationships that a woman shares with a man.

The section includes one of the most graphic warnings against adultery to be found in the Bible. The language of the teaching is so blunt that there is no chance of mistaking the gravity of sexual sin:

> He who commits adultery has no sense;
>   he who does it destroys himself.
> Wounds and dishonor will he get,
>   and his disgrace will not be wiped away.
>   *(6:32, 33, Revised*
>   *Standard Version)*

Then follows (7:6-27) an absolutely unforgettable description of a man who is seduced by a harlot, until—

> He goeth after her straightway
>   as an ox goeth to the slaughter,
> Or as a fool to the correction of the stocks;
>   Till a dart strike through his liver. . . .

>Her house is the way to hell,
>> going down to the chambers of death.
>>> *(7:22, 23, 27)*

More Proverbs of Solomon

The second section of Proverbs, also identified as belonging to Solomon, deals with the contrasts in life, especially in righteous and evil living. These proverbs are more mundane than previous statements of wisdom and folly.

>The memory of the just is blessed:
>But the name of the wicked shall rot.
>> *(10:7)*

>Hatred stirreth up strifes:
>But love covereth all sins.
>> *(10:12)*

Discretion is a popular virtue, mentioned frequently in this section:

>As a jewel of gold in a swine's snout,
>So is a fair woman which is without discretion.
>> *(11:22)*

>He that keepeth his mouth keepeth his life:
>But he that openeth wide his lips shall have
>> destruction.
>>> *(13:3)*

>Whoso keepeth his mouth and his tongue
>keepeth his soul from troubles.
>> *(21:23)*

Third Section

The third section is introduced in chapter 22:17 as being "words of the wise," with no further identification of who "the wise" might be. This set of parables speaks frequently in severe terms, with pungent warnings and counsel. Among its severe warnings is this much quoted statement against drunkenness:

> Who hath woe? Who hath sorrow?
> Who hath contentions? Who hath babbling?
> Who hath wounds without cause?
> Who hath redness of eyes?
>> They that tarry long at the wine;
>> they that go to seek mixed wine.
> Look not thou upon the wine when it is red,
>> when it giveth its color in the cup,
>> when it moveth itself aright.
> At the last it biteth like a serpent,
>> and stingeth like an adder.
>
> *(23:29-32)*

Fourth Section

The fourth section consists of still more proverbs of Solomon; they were not collected for reading until the reign of Hezekiah. These are simpler and more direct than the earlier two sets by Solomon.

Proverbs of Agur

The fifth section of Proverbs brings a change of style and substance from all the others. It is identified as the work of a man called Agur, the son of Jakeh; but the further notation, "the man spake unto Ithiel, even unto Ithiel and Ucal" has no meaning for us today. We have no further clues concerning the identity of Agur.

The whole tone of this collection of proverbs is different from the others. Agur exalts the wisdom of God and, with a series of related examples, shows that the wisdom of men cannot approach the wisdom of God. Men do not have the wisdom or ability to fathom God's secrets, unless God reveals His wisdom to men.

Every word of God is pure:
>   he is a shield unto them that put their trust in
>   him.
Add thou not unto his words,
>   lest he reprove thee, and thou be found a liar.
Two things have I required of thee;
>   deny me them not before I die:
Remove far from me vanity and lies;
>   give me neither poverty nor riches;
>   feed me with food convenient for me,
Lest I be full, and deny thee,
>   and say, "Who is the LORD?"
or lest I be poor, and steal,
>   and take the name of my God in vain.

(30:5-9)

In a series of "numerical" proverbs, so called because of Agur's device of numbering, he carries the deficiency of man's understanding further:

There be three things which are too wonderful for
>   me;
>   yea, four which I know not:
The way of an eagle in the air;
>   the way of a serpent upon a rock;
the way of a ship in the midst of the sea;
>   and the way of a man with a maid.

(30:18, 19)

The Crowning Proverbs

The sixth section of Proverbs is introduced as "The words of King Lemuel, the prophecy that his mother taught him." No hint is given as to who Lemuel might be, though some scholars identify him as an Arabian king whose proverbs were taken over by the Israelites. The group that originated with Lemuel's mother (verses 2-9) warns against the folly of lust and strong drink for a king:

It is not for kings, O Lemuel,
    it is not for kings to drink wine;
    nor for princes strong drink;

(31:4)

The short section seems to be instructions given by a mother to a son who would be king.

There is an abrupt change at 31:10, where a sublime portrait of ideal womanhood begins. It is one of the rarest literary gems in Scripture, an acrostic poem that begins each couplet with a letter of the Hebrew alphabet. *The Dartmouth Bible* says:

This passage is worthy of note not only because of its striking conception of woman's role but also because it is regarded by some as the finest of the fourteen examples of acrostic (alphabetic) poetry in the Old Testament. In the Hebrew Bible these twenty-two parallelistic couplets each begin with words in which the first letters are successively the letters of the Hebrew alphabet.

The world is made richer by this elegant composition that extols the character of a worthy woman. With the inspired writer, we can also say:

Favor is deceitful, and beauty is vain:
    but a woman that feareth the Lord, she shall
    be praised.
Give her of the fruit of her hands;
    and let her own works praise her in the gates.

(31:30, 31)

ECCLESIASTES

The Book of Ecclesiastes or, the Preacher, is a statement of religious cynicism. It is one of those instances of which Dr. Hassell Bullock says: "Although the Hebrew-Christian tradition has required faith of its adherents, it has recognized that life and faith have their high and low attitudes, and sometimes out of doubt and skepticism faith is born and nourished" (*An Introduction to the Old Testament Poetic Books*).

Known as Qoheleth, or Koheleth, in the Hebrew Bible, Ecclesiastes seems to be the work of Solomon (1:1). By use of the phrase "under the sun" he constantly reminds us that these are the skeptical views of natural man.

> Vanity of vanities, saith the Preacher,
>   vanity of vanities;
>   all is vanity.
> What profit hath a man of all his labor
>   which he taketh under the sun?
>
> *(1:2, 3)*

If Solomon expressed joy in the Song of Solomon and faith in Proverbs, he expresses pessimism in Ecclesiastes. He had sought happiness in various ways, yet had come away empty so often that he was disillusioned and cynical (2:1). What the writer of Ecclesiastes was, Job could easily have become. In that sense, Ecclesiastes is the reverse side of spiritual optimism and hope found elsewhere, what we might call "the other side of the coin."

God obviously wants us to learn the lessons that come from pessimism, for even disillusioned and skeptical men need to be understood. We need to see their point of view.

Divisions of the Book

There are three natural divisions in the book, in which, while there is no change of mood, we do see a difference in style.

1. The proposition that all is vanity (chapters 1-3)
2. The view that happiness and satisfaction are not to be found on earth (chapters 4-10)
3. The conclusion that only in God can peace and happiness be found (chapters 11, 12)

The emphasis in the first section is Solomon's inability to find contentment in such advantages as a pleasant environment (2:4-6), material possessions (2:7, 8), pleasures (2:8), wisdom (2:9), self-indulgence (2:10), and personal achievement (2:10, 11). These left Solomon empty and unfulfilled; he said, "Behold, all was vanity and vexation of spirit, and there was no profit under the sun" (2:11).

The second section carries the proposition further, but the Preacher extends his pessimism beyond his personal experience and makes its encompass the whole of mankind. In this, cynicism finds its lowest point:

For there is not a just man upon earth, that doeth good, and sinneth not.

(7:20)

This is an evil among all things that are done under the sun, that there is one event unto all; yea, also the heart of the sons of men is full of evil, and madness is in their heart while they live, and after that they go to the dead.

(9:3)

The final division allows a crack in the granite facade of pessimism, and a ray of hope appears. In a series of proverbs, Solomon acknowledges that although evil still prevails, good men must make the best of it and expect good to come of their efforts. The Preacher maintains his view that all is vanity (12:8) but concludes with this admonition:

Let us hear the conclusion of the whole matter: Fear God,
and keep his commandments; for this is the whole duty of
man. For God shall bring every work into judgment, with
every secret thing, whether it be good, or whether it be evil.

(12:13, 14)

LAMENTATIONS OF JEREMIAH

The Book of Lamentations is probably the least-
read, least-appreciated book in the Bible. It is a series
of five laments, or dirges, over Jerusalem's fall to the
Babylonians. The book's lack of appeal is due to its
doleful nature and unattractive title. As the modern
poet, Emma Wheeler Wilcox says in her poem, "The
Way of the World,"

> Laugh, and the world laughs with you,
> Weep, and you weep alone,
> For the brave old earth must borrow its mirth—
> But has trouble enough of its own.
> Sing, and the hills will answer,
> Sigh, it is lost on the air;
> The echoes rebound to a joyful sound
> And shrink from voicing care.

The Book of Lamentations is a highly literate work
of great beauty and exquisite pathos, but its subject
matter is melancholy and sad. For reasons not clear,
except that he was known as the Weeping Prophet,
the poem has long been associated with the name of
Jeremiah. But mourning has been a feature of Jewish
expression from time immemorial. (Jewish music is
often in a minor key, and the Wailing Wall has long
been a prominent feature of Jerusalem.)

The Desolate City

The opening lines of Lamentations set the theme of
all five laments:

> How doth the city sit solitary,
>   that was full of people!
> How is she become as a widow!
>   she that was great among the nations,
>   and princess among the provinces,
> How is she become tributary!
>
> She weepeth sore in the night,
>   and her tears are on her cheeks.
> Among all her lovers
>   she hath none to comfort her;
> all her friends have dealt treacherously with her,
>   they are become her enemies.
>
> *(1:1, 2)*

Israel's attachment to the city of Jerusalem exceeds that of any city/nation relationship of the Western world. It was believed that divine grace was associated with the Holy City. (In today's news, we can see that it is still the same!) Even the prophets of Israel were hindered in their work as long as Jerusalem was desolate:

> . . . her prophets also find
> no vision from the Lord.
> The elders of the daughter of Zion
>   sit upon the ground and keep silence:
> they have cast dust upon their heads;
>   they have girded themselves with sackcloth.
>
> *(2:9, 10)*

Reasons for the Fall

The laments over Jerusalem were not exercises in futility, however, for the songs of mourning sought the reasons for their desolation. In the First Lament, we read of the sins of the city:

> Jerusalem hath grievously sinned;
>   therefore she is removed:

> all that honoured her despise her,
>> because they have seen her nakedness:
> Yea, she sigheth, and turneth backward.
>> *(1:8)*

and Jerusalem herself confesses:

> My yoke of my transgressions is bound by his hand:
> They are wreathed, and come upon my neck:
>> he hath made my strength to fall,
> The Lord hath delivered me into their hands,
>> from whom I am not able to rise up. . . .
> The Lord is righteous;
>> for I have rebelled against his commandment:
> Hear, I pray you, all people,
>> and behold my sorrow:
> my virgins and my young men
>> are gone into captivity.
>>> *(1:14, 18)*

In the Second and Fourth Laments, sins of the religious leaders are exposed:

> Thy prophets have seen vain and foolish things for
>> thee:
> and they have not discovered thine iniquity,
>> to turn away thy captivity;
> but have seen for thee false burdens
>> and causes of banishment.
>>> *(2:14)*

> For the sins of her prophets,
>> and the iniquities of her priests,
> that have shed the blood of the just
>> in the midst of her.
>>> *(4:13)*

The Book of Lamentations rises to heights of prophetic pathos, with a final lament, the Fifth, that sounds like a cry in many parts of our troubled world today:

> We are orphans and fatherless,
>   our mothers are as widows. . . .
> Our necks are under persecution:
>   we labour and have no rest. . . .
> Our fathers have sinned, and are not;
>   and we have borne their iniquities. . . .
> The crown is fallen from our head:
>   woe unto us, that we have sinned!
> For this our heart is faint;
>   for these things our eyes are dim.
>
> *(5:3, 5, 7, 16, 17)*

Even in deep sorrow, mankind has gained great beauty, which, after all, is one reason for the chastening of the Lord.

DISCUSSION QUESTIONS

1. Explain what a maxim is. What book in the Scriptures was most characterized by this style of writing?

2. By whom were the Proverbs written? Study the six natural divisions of the Book of Proverbs and identify the author of each.

3. How do you relate the picture of ideal womanhood in Proverbs 31 to the Christian woman of today?

4. What do you feel is the true message of the Book of Ecclesiastes as it applies to all of us?

5. The Book of Lamentations expresses grief over the plight of a great city, Jerusalem. Why was the condition of this city of such importance to Israel?

Spokesmen 5
for God

There were two kinds of spiritual leaders in Israel: priests and prophets. Although they both represented God to the people, they were quite different in two important ways. First, the priests were responsible for religious ritual and ceremony, and the prophets were responsible for evangelism and preaching. Second, the priests, being Levites, were ministers by birth, and the prophets were individually called of God for particular service in times of need.

The prophets were a particular breed of men, anointed of God to speak for Him, especially in times of national crisis. They were fired by a zeal for righteousness rather than ceremony, as Samuel once emphasized to King Saul:

> Hath the LORD as great delight in burnt offerings
> and sacrifices,
> as in obeying the voice of the LORD?
> Behold, to obey is better than sacrifice,
> and to hearken than the fat of rams.
>
> *(1 Samuel 15:22)*

The fervid nature of a prophet's calling and ministry is seen in Jeremiah's account of his anointing:

> Then the LORD put forth his hand, and touched my
> mouth. And the LORD said unto me,
> Behold, I have put my words in thy mouth.

See, I have this day set thee over the nations
    and over the kingdoms,
to root out, and to pull down,
and to destroy and to throw down,
to build, and to plant.

(Jeremiah 1:9, 10)

Then I said, I will not make mention of him,
    nor speak any more in his name.
But his word was in mine heart as a burning fire
    shut up in my bones,
and I was weary with forbearing,
    and I could not stay.

(Jeremiah 20:9)

There were many prophets, more than could ever
be enumerated. We read of them in plural terms that
suggest great numbers (see Numbers 11:29, 1 Kings
22:6, 2 Kings 2:7, 2 Kings 3:13). A considerable
number of prophets are mentioned by name in the
Scriptures:

Aaron, Exodus 7:1	Medad, Numbers 11:26
Abraham, Genesis 20:7	Moses, Deuteronomy
David, Matthew 13:35	34:10
Eldad, Numbers 11:26	Nathan, 1 Kings 1:32
Elijah, 1 Kings 18:26	Oded, 2 Chronicles 15:8
Elisha, 2 Kings 6:8	Samuel, Acts 3:25
Gad, 1 Samuel 22:5	Iddo, 2 Chronicles 13:22
Hananiah, Jeremiah	Jehu, 1 Kings 16:7
28:17	Shemaiah, 2 Chronicles
Ahijah, 1 Kings 11:29	12:5
Balaam, Numbers 24:2	Micaiah, 1 Kings 22:8
Joshua, 1 Kings 16:34	Agabus, Acts 21:10

Significantly, some women were also called into prophetic service. The prophetesses mentioned by name
were:

Deborah, Judges 4:4   Noadiah, Nehemiah 6:14
Huldah, 2 Kings 22:14   Anna, Luke 2:36
Miriam, Exodus 15:20   Philip's daughters,
                           Acts 21:9

WORK OF THE PROPHETS

Most of the prophets mentioned by name have
something of their work recorded also, which helps us
to see the purposes they fulfilled. Such men as Abraham,
Moses, David, Joshua and Samuel are so well known
for other reasons that we tend to forget that they were
prophets, but the others had strictly prophetic minis-
tries of varied results and under varied circumstances.
For instance:

Nathan is known chiefly, if not altogether, for his
confrontation with King David when the latter had
grievously sinned with Bathsheba, wife of Uriah. Nathan's
courage, and his dramatic disclosure of David's sin are
a remarkable example of prophetic purpose.

Elijah, whose long ministry spanned about thirty
years of Hebrew history, is known for so many powerful works that he could be called an Old Testament
apostle. His challenge of the prophets of Baal is an
example of prophetic daring against humanly impos-
sible odds. His conflict with King Ahab and Jezebel
was a remarkable example of the superiority of spiritual power over temporal power.

Elisha, successor to Elijah, was even more effective
than his mentor, but does not hold the popular
imagination of Elijah, due no doubt to the fact that
Elijah was the prophetic trailblazer of that period.

Micaiah was one of the most interesting of the
prophets. God used him in a very special way when
Ahab, king of Israel, sought the alliance of Jehoshaphat,

king of Judah, in a military campaign against Ramoth-gilead. Ahab and Jehoshaphat sought the counsel of four hundred prophets who seem to have been advisors in Ahab's court (1 Kings 22:5, 6), who gave the answer the king desired: "Go up to Ramoth-gilead and prosper: for the Lord shall deliver it into the King's hand."

Jehoshaphat, not convinced by the pat assurances, asked if another prophet were available, to which Ahab replied: "There is yet one man, Micaiah the son of Imlah, by whom we may inquire of the Lord; but I hate him; for he doth not prophesy good concerning me, but evil."

When Micaiah was brought in, he mocked the king, first by parroting what the other prophets had said, and then with a satirical story that showed that they were influenced by a lying spirit. Micaiah finally revealed that Ahab would be killed if he went to battle. The prophecy was true and Ahab was killed.

FALSE PROPHETS

This account highlights the fact that Israel had many false prophets as well as the true. Such prophets as Isaiah, Jeremiah, Ezekiel and Micah spoke vigorously against these pretenders. Isaiah said that they "prophesy not unto us right things" but that they prophesy "smooth things" and "deceits" (Isaiah 30:10).

Jeremiah said, "The prophets prophesy falsely" (Jeremiah 5:31), and Ezekiel used much more colorful language: "And her prophets have daubed them with untempered (whitewash, *RSV*) mortar, seeing vanity, and divining lies unto them, saying, Thus saith the Lord God, when the Lord hath not spoken" (Ezekiel 22:28).

Micah, speaking to both Judah and Israel, spoke of "prophets that make my people err" and continued with these condemning words:

> "And the sun shall go down over the prophets,
>   and the day shall be dark over them.
> Then shall the seers be ashamed,
>   and the diviners confounded."

Then speaking of Jerusalem, he said:

> "The priests thereof teach for hire,
> and the prophets thereof divine for money:
> Yet will they lean upon the Lord, and say,
>   Is not the Lord among us?
>   None evil can come upon us."
>
> *(Micah 3:6, 7, 11)*

THE NATURE OF PROPHECY

True prophecy was given under the influence of the Spirit of God, as we note from such phrases as:
"The Lord hath spoken,"
"thus saith the Lord,"
"saith your God,"
"God doth instruct him,"
"the mouth of the Lord hath spoken it,"
"the word of the Lord came unto me, saying,"
and numerous others. It is clear that the prophet was indeed a spokesman for the Lord.

Most prophecy was sermonic or denunciatory in nature, calling the people to repentance when they erred from the ways of God. The work of the prophet had much more to do with the here and now than with the future, although it is commonly, and incorrectly, felt that all prophecy is futuristic. The idea that all prophecy has some mystical reference to the future is unfortunate for it keeps many persons from the enjoyment of eloquent arguments for righteousness and exposures of sin.

There are visions of the future in some of the prophetic books, to be sure, but for the greater part we read of such things as this appeal of Isaiah:

"Seek ye the Lord while he may be found,
　　call ye upon him while he is near:
Let the wicked forsake his way,
　　and the unrighteous man his thoughts:
and let him return unto the Lord, and he will
　　　　have mercy upon him;
　　and to our God, for he will abundantly pardon.

For my thoughts are not your thoughts,
　　neither are your ways my ways, saith the Lord.
For as the heavens are higher than the earth,
so are my ways higher than your ways,
　　and my thoughts than your thoughts.
For as the rain cometh down,
　　and the snow from heaven,
and returneth not thither, but watereth the earth,
　　and maketh it bring forth and bud,
that it may give seed to the sower,
　　and bread to the eater:
So shall my word be that goeth forth out of my
　　　　mouth:
　　it shall not return unto me void,
but it shall accomplish that which I please,
　　and it shall prosper in the thing whereto I sent
　　　　it.

　　　　　　　　　　　　　(Isaiah 55:6-11)

PROPHETS WHO WROTE

Some of the greatest prophets, such as Elijah and Elisha, never committed their prophecies to writing; they were not literary men and left no recorded sermons or books. The prophetic message was principally an oral message, intended for proclamation rather than writing, and effecting immediate rather than delayed responses.

But there were sixteen prophets who did write, and it is from their writings that we learn most about the prophetic ministry. Of the sixteen, four are called Major Prophets, for no reason except the length of their writings. These are:

Isaiah	Ezekiel
Jeremiah	Daniel

Twelve are called Minor Prophets, not because they were less important or effective than those called Major, but because their writings were shorter. These are:

Hosea	Nahum
Joel	Habakkuk
Amos	Zephaniah
Obadiah	Haggai
Jonah	Zechariah
Micah	Malachi

These sixteen literary prophets lived over a period of approximately 425 years, which covered a large, important stretch of Israelite history. It is interesting to read the prophets' writings in the order that they lived, for then we see the circumstances of their work more clearly. According to the studies of several Old Testament scholars, although reference points are too scarce to fix dates with certainty, the following sequence of the prophets seems fairly accurate:

DIVISION OF THE KINGDOM, c. 930 B.C.

Obadiah	(of Judah)	c. 845	(to Edom)
Joel	(of Judah)	c. 835	(to Judah)
Jonah	(of Israel)	c. 782-765	(to Nineveh)

Hosea	(of Israel)	c. 760-725	(to Israel and Judah)
Amos	(of Judah)	c. 760	(to Israel)
Isaiah	(of Judah)	c. 739	(to Judah)
Micah	(of Judah)	c. 735-725	(to Judah and Israel)

CONQUEST OF ISRAEL BY ASSYRIA, c. 721 B.C.

Nahum	(of Judah)	c. 650-612	(to Nineveh)
Zephaniah	(of Judah)	c. 640-608	(to Judah)
Jeremiah	(of Judah)	c. 627	(to Judah)
Habakkuk	(of Judah)	c. 609	(to Judah)

DEPORTATION OF JEWS TO BABYLON, c. 605 B.C.

| Daniel | (of Babylon) | c. 605-535 | (to Babylon) |
| Ezekiel | (of Babylon) | c. 597 | (to Jewish exiles) |

RESTORATION OF JEWISH HOMELAND, c. 536 B.C.

Haggai	(of Judah)	c. 520	(to Judah)
Zechariah	(of Judah)	c. 520-510	(to Judah)
Malachi	(of Judah)	c. 433-420	(to Judah)

It should be emphasized that there is no way of dating the work of individual prophets with unquestioned certainty. Such dating is a tedious process of comparing persons and circumstances mentioned in the books with known historical dates and records.

The prophets who wrote books all lived after David and Solomon's united kingdom was divided into the Southern Kingdom (Judah) under Rehoboam and the Northern Kingdom (Israel) under Jeroboam in 930 B.C. Seven of the prophets came before the conquest of the Northern Kingdom by Assyria in 721 B.C. Four others lived during the 150 years that the Southern Kingdom survived alone, before Judah was conquered and its people taken to Babylon in 597 B.C.

Two prophets preached during the exile in Babylon. The Jews were restored to their homeland in 536 B.C., after which three final prophets did their work. This is how we will now survey the sixteen individual prophets, for we need to observe these spokesmen for God in the chronological order of their great work.

1. *The Pre-exilic Prophets* (eleven)
   Obadiah, Joel, Jonah, Hosea, Amos
   Isaiah, Micah, Nahum, Zephaniah, Jeremiah, Habakkuk

2. *Prophets of the Exile* (two)
   Daniel, Ezekiel

3. *Prophets of the Restoration* (three)
   Haggai, Zechariah, Malachi

DISCUSSION QUESTIONS

1. Explain the differences in the two kinds of spiritual leaders in Israel: priests and prophets.

2. Enumerate some of the major works of Elijah; of Elisha. How do you compare these two outstanding prophets?

3. What was the primary nature and purpose of the message of these prophets of Israel?

4. Of the sixteen prophets who wrote, four were called Major Prophets and twelve were called Minor Prophets. Name these and explain why they were so called.

5. In what way does the message of these prophets of Israel have meaning for us today?

The Early 6
Prophets

All of the canonical prophets (those whose books are included in the Bible) lived after the Jewish nation was divided into the kingdoms of Judah and Israel. Most of the prophecies were directed to only one of the kingdoms, but, as we shall see, some prophets spoke to both. Some of the prophets reached further still and preached to neighboring lands such as Edom, Moab and Philistia. The men preached wherever and to whomever God led them.

The earliest writing prophet wrote of a tragedy that happened to Judah, but his principal message was to Edom, who had dealt evilly with Judah. The prophet's name was Obadiah.

OBADIAH

The prophecy of Obadiah is not only the earliest but also the shortest written prophecy—only one chapter of twenty-one verses. We know little or nothing about Obadiah himself, but the subject of his writing is familiar indeed: It is as old as the Jewish nation and as current as today's newspaper. He spoke about the sins of Edom against Judah.

The Edomites were descendants of Esau, which made them kinsmen of the Israelites, who were descended from Jacob. It also made them enemies.

The Edomites had strongly resisted the Jews' original settlement in Canaan, but lived side by side in a kind of peace with them after Israel became a nation.

The inherent enmity reasserted itself, however, at a time of national disaster for Judah, when Edom added to the Jews' distress. When Jehoram was king of Judah, the nation was attacked by the Philistines and Arabians; Jerusalem was pillaged and its people either fled, or were taken captive, or were killed. Edom not only refused to assist Judah but also took advantage of their distress to join in the plunder of Jerusalem. They betrayed the refugees from Jerusalem, helped sack the city and even seized a part of Judah's territory.

So Obadiah spoke against Edom in the bitterest terms:

> But thou shouldest not have looked on the day of
>   thy brother
> In the day that he became a stranger;
> Neither shouldest thou have rejoiced over the children
>   of Judah
> In the day of their destruction;
> Neither shouldest thou have spoken proudly
> In the day of distress.
> Thou shouldest not have entered into the gate of my
>   people
> In the day of their calamity;
> Yea, thou shouldest not have looked on their affliction
> In the day of their calamity,
> Nor have laid hands on their substance
> In the day of their calamity;
> Neither shouldest thou have stood in the crossway,
> To cut off those of his that did escape;
> Neither shouldest thou have delivered up those of his
> That did remain in the day of distress.
>
> *(1:12-14)*

Obadiah foretold that Edom itself would be attacked
and destroyed for their treachery against Jacob:

> For thy violence against thy brother Jacob,
>   shame shall cover thee,
>   and thou shalt be cut off for ever . . .
> For the day of the LORD is near upon all the heathen:
> As thou hast done, it shall be done unto thee:
>   thy reward shall return upon thine own head.
>
> *(1:10, 15)*

As foretold, Edom was soon defeated and the nation lost its identity as a people. Remnants of the
Edomites became known as Idumeans, from whom
came Herod the Great, usurper of the throne of
David at the time of Christ's birth. Those descendants
of Esau have now dissolved into a spreading Arabic
world that carries on an unending fight against Israel.
The conclusion of the matter, which is yet to come, is
graphically described by Obadiah:

> The house of Jacob shall be a fire,
>   and the house of Joseph a flame,
>   and the house of Esau for stubble;
> And they shall kindle in them, and devour them;
> And there shall not be any remaining
>   of the house of Esau;
> For the Lord hath spoken it.
>
> *(1:18)*

JOEL

The prophet Joel also lived in Judah at the same
time as Obadiah, which was about the time that Elijah
was active farther north in Israel. Joel's written prophecy was motivated by a devastating plague of locusts
that invaded the land like a vicious army and stripped
the country of its vegetation.

For a nation is come up upon my land,
    strong, and without number,
whose teeth are the teeth of a lion,
    and he hath the cheek teeth of a great lion.
He hath laid my vine waste,
    and barked my fig tree:
he hath made it clean bare, and cast it away;
    the branches thereof are made white.

(1:6, 7)

Joel spoke of the different varieties of locusts that had brought about the disaster, as we read in the *Revised Standard Version*:

What the cutting locust left,
    the swarming locust has eaten.
What the swarming locust left,
    the hopping locust has eaten,
and what the hopping locust left,
    the destroying locust has eaten.

(1:4, Revised
Standard Version)

The calamity included the destruction of orchards, vineyards, olive groves and cultivated fields. Even the cattle and sheep died for lack of pasturage. This, in turn, eliminated the animals as sacrifices, so worship in the temple had been suspended (1:10, 13, 18).

Joel urgently appealed to the people to repent of their sins, to fast and pray unto the Lord:

Sanctify ye a fast,
    call a solemn assembly.
Gather the elders
    and all the inhabitants of the land
into the house of the LORD your God;
    and cry unto the LORD. . . .

(1:14)

> Therefore also now, saith the LORD,
> turn ye even to me with all your heart,
> And with fasting, and with weeping, and with
>   mourning. . . .
>
> *(2:12)*

Out of the disaster came hope. Joel emphasized the forgiving nature of God and stated that the locusts would be blown into the desert and out to sea (2:20). Most wonderful of all was the promise of a renewal of God's Holy Spirit:

> And it shall come to pass afterward,
> that I will pour out my Spirit upon all flesh;
> And your sons and your daughters shall prophesy,
>   your old men shall dream dreams,
>   your young men shall see visions:
> And also upon the servants and upon the handmaids
>   in those days will I pour out my Spirit.
>
> *(2:28, 29)*

These words of Joel were repeated by Peter on the Day of Pentecost, with an explanation that the Pentecostal outpouring of the Holy Spirit was a fulfillment of the promise (Acts 2:16-21). Furthermore, the Pentecostal renewal is to continue on earth until the actual "last days"—when the "day of the Lord" shall come to the earth.

Joel 3 is a survey of the sins that will bring the judgment of God upon the earth in the last days, which will be a triumphant day for all followers of God—

> The LORD also shall roar out of Zion,
>   and utter his voice from Jerusalem;
> and the heavens and the earth shall shake:
>   but the Lord will be the hope of his people,
>   and the strength of the children of Israel.
>
> *(3:16)*

All men who put their hope and trust in the Lord can look for His coming with great confidence and hope. That is the privilege of His people today.

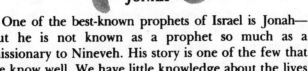

JONAH

One of the best-known prophets of Israel is Jonah—but he is not known as a prophet so much as a missionary to Nineveh. His story is one of the few that we know well. We have little knowledge about the lives of Obadiah, Nahum, Micah and others, but we know a great deal about Jonah. Although we have some facts about Ezekiel, Amos, Isaiah and Jeremiah, we know still more about Jonah. Only Daniel equals the prophet Jonah in our knowledge of him. Most of the Book of Jonah is an account of his mission to Nineveh.

Because of this fact, the story is believed by many Bible critics to be fiction. But Jonah was real enough: we have Jesus' word for that (Matthew 12:39-41). He was an actual historical person and the events related in his book really happened.

Jonah, who belonged to the Northern Kingdom of Israel, was called by the Lord to go to Nineveh, the capital city of Assyria, one of the great cities of the world at that time (1:2). But he was reluctant to preach to a non-Jewish people. He furthermore believed that even after he preached to Nineveh God would show mercy to the idolatrous people and spare them (4:2), which would then make his prophecy vain. The prophet therefore fled from his calling by embarking upon a ship bound for Tarshish, across the Mediterranean Sea.

A series of miracles then occurred that forced Jonah to Nineveh. First, a storm so battered the ship that the sailors cast lots to see who was responsible for the

furious sea. When the lot correctly indicated it was
Jonah, he was thrown overboard, where he would
have drowned except for a great fish that rescued him
and kept him safe for three days.

No story in the Bible has been more analyzed,
criticized and debated than that story of the fish.
There is no need to fuss over the size of whales'
esophaguses, for it was a special fish prepared for the
specific purpose (1:17). The same One who caused the
wind also prepared the fish. Inside the fish, Jonah
prayed an earnest prayer (2:1-9) and the fish vomited
the prophet onto dry land.

The Lord's call to preach in Nineveh was repeated,
and Jonah obeyed. Nineveh was so vast that it required
three days to see it all. There Jonah preached for one
day—a message that consisted of exactly eight words:

> "Yet forty days,
>   and Nineveh shall be overthrown."
>
> *(3:4)*

Jonah preached his brief message with such power
and conviction that the city, from the king down,
fasted and repented in sackcloth and ashes (ancient
symbols of humiliation). God spared the city when he
saw the people's repentance. That eventuality, although
anticipated by Jonah, greatly displeased him because
he wanted to see the ruthless, idolatrous city destroyed
(4:1). But the possibility of repentance and salvation
was, after all, the purpose behind God's sending
Jonah to Nineveh. That is still the possibility and
purpose behind all preaching.

The Lord was as gracious to His unhappy prophet
as He had been to the Ninevites. When Nineveh was
not destroyed at the end of forty days, Jonah, who

could have seemed like a false prophet, prayed that he
might die (4:3), but God dealt gently with him in a
way he could understand. A gourd plant grew
miraculously and sheltered Jonah at the edge of the
city. Jonah appreciated its shade, but God prepared a
worm that caused the plant to die. Without the favor-
able shelter, Jonah suffered from a searing windstorm
and the broiling Assyrian sun (4:6-8).

God then patiently explained to His prophet that
just as Jonah grieved over the death of the gourd, so
He, the Lord, would have grieved over the death of
Nineveh with 120,000 innocent children in it (4:11),
which is what the expression "cannot discern between
their right hand and their left hand" means.

HOSEA

The prophetic ministry of Hosea extended over a
period of forty years—and some scholars suggest that
it may have been as long as sixty to sixty-five years.
He ministered to the Northern Kingdom of Israel at
the time Amos also preached there, and Isaiah and
Micah preached in Judah. Happily, Hosea dates his
book with the list of kings who reigned while he was
in the prophetic office. It was a time of widespread
apostasy in both kingdoms, as all those prophets'
books reveal.

The Book of Hosea is in two divisions that we need
to observe in order to understand its message. The
first, chapters 1-3, consists of a narrative on Hosea's
marriage to an adulterous wife. The second, chapters
4-14, consists of sermons Hosea preached to Israel, in
which he frequently used his own marriage to illus-
trate the religious adultery of the nation. It was a
wicked time when political and spiritual conspiracy
knew no limits:

Hear the word of the Lord, ye children of Israel;
for the Lord hath a controversy with the inhabitants of
    the land.
Because there is no truth, nor mercy,
    nor knowledge of God in the land.
By swearing, and lying, and killing, and stealing, and
    committing adultery:
    they break out and blood touches blood.
Therefore shall the land mourn,
    and everyone that dwelleth therein shall languish,
    with the beasts of the field,
    and with the fowls of heaven;
    yea, the fishes of the sea shall be taken away.
                          (4:1-3)

In order to speak to so wicked a time, God directed
Hosea to make himself a living example of love and
compassion by marrying a harlot. So the prophet
married Gomer, who bore him two sons and a daughter. Gomer's whoredoms included the sexual orgies of
Baal and Ashtoreth and an elopement with adulterous
lovers (2:13). Hosea went after his faithless wife following one of her escapades and paid a ransom of
silver and barley for her release from her lover and
return to him (3:2). This demonstrated the love of the
Lord for the adulterous nation of Israel, who had
forsaken Him to worship other gods. Yet He had paid
a ransom for their return to Him.

The idolatry in the Northern Kingdom was in
evidence everywhere, and it spread into the Southern
Kingdom as well (5:5, 10; 6:4, 11). Both kingdoms—
but Israel in particular—forsook God and formed
alliances with heathen lands:

Ephraim also is like a silly dove without heart:
    they call to Egypt, they go to Assyria. . . .
                    (7:11)

> For they are gone up to Assyria,
>   a wild ass alone by himself:
> Ephraim hath hired lovers.
>
> (8:9)

The pain in the Father's heart is seen as He recalls His tender care of the people when they were young, in some of the most poignant words in all the Word of God:

> When Israel was a child, I loved him,
>   and out of Egypt I called my son.
> The more I called them,
>   the more they went from me,
> they kept sacrificing to the Baals,
>   and burning incense to idols.
> Yet it was I who taught Ephraim to walk,
>   I took them up in my arms;
>   but they did not know that I healed them.
> I led them with cords of compassion,
>   with the bands of love,
> and I became to them as one
>   who eases the yoke on their jaws,
>   and I bent down to them and fed them.
>
> (11:1-4, Revised
Standard Version)

The prophecy of Hosea concludes with God appealing to His people to return to Him. They did not know that they were destroying themselves and paid no heed to God's love for them.

The prophecy is one of the most touching in the Old Testament; it succeeds in conveying divine compassion in human terms, for in Hosea we can see God very well.

AMOS

Amos, one of the most colorful of the pre-exilic prophets, was one of those sturdy, forthright individuals that make us proud of the human race. He was as rugged as the countryside of Tekoa, a region south of Jerusalem where he tended his sheep and groomed his vineyards. He was what we might call a "country boy," rough and unlettered. He came from no illustrious family, so his father's name is not mentioned; Amos said of himself, "I was no prophet, neither was I a prophet's son; but I was an herdman, and a gatherer of sycomore fruit: and the Lord took me as I followed the flock, and the Lord said unto me, Go, prophesy unto my people Israel" (7:14, 15).

These words were occasioned when Amaziah, the apostate priest of Bethel, criticized Amos for coming from Judah to preach in Israel. Amos' retort was that it was God who had called him to prophesy in Israel. The forceful prophet began his ministry in a way that would make any people shudder:

> The Lord will roar from Zion,
>   and utter his voice from Jerusalem;
> And the habitations of the shepherds shall mourn,
>   and the top of Carmel shall wither.
> Will a lion roar in the forest,
>   when he hath no prey?
> Will a young lion cry out of his den
>   if he have taken nothing?
> The lion hath roared,
>   who will not fear?
> The LORD God hath spoken,
>   who can but prophesy?
>
>   *(1:2; 3:4, 8)*

Amos preached in Israel during the reigns of Uzziah in Judah and Jeroboam II in Israel, a time of affluence and prosperity in both kingdoms. The material well-being had come at great cost, however, for moral degeneracy was rampant in Israel. The leaders of the Northern Kingdom were guilty of oppression and injustice, and the people were guilty of greed, dishonesty and immorality. The burden of Amos' ministry was against those evils, with special emphasis on injustice.

The book opens with a series of eight judgments against six surrounding nations—Damascus (1:3-5), Gaza (1:6-8), Tyre (1:9, 10), Edom (1:11, 12), Ammon (1:13-15), and Moab (2:1-3)—plus Judah (2:4, 5), and Israel (2:6-16). These prophecies of judgment deserve close study, in view of the guilt involved and the penalties to be exacted for the guilt.

Most of Amos' message is to those who are wealthy, powerful and self-righteous, who have afflicted others for personal gain and benefit.

> Hear this word, you cows of Bashan,
>   who are in the mountain of Samaria,
> who oppress the poor, who crush the needy,
>   who say to their husbands, Bring, that we may
>   drink!
> The Lord GOD has sworn by his holiness
>   that, behold, the days are coming upon you,
> when they shall take you away with hooks,
>   even the last of you with fishhooks.
>
>   *(4:1, 2, Revised*
>   *Standard Version)*

The forceful, blunt language of Amos, such as calling the wealthy women cows, mark him as a plain man of the people who was touched with the prophetic fire. Consider these stinging words to the hypocrites who oppressed the poor, lived by wickedness and still went through the pretenses of religion. Such worship, says Amos, is an insult to God! The prophet fearlessly quotes the Lord as saying:

> I hate, I despise your feast days,
>> and I will not smell in your solemn assemblies.
> Though ye offer me burnt offerings and your
>> meat offerings,
>> I will not accept them;
> Neither will I regard the peace offerings
>> of your fat beasts.
> Take away from me the noise of thy songs;
>> for I will not hear the melody of your viols.
> But let judgment run down as waters,
>> and righteousness as a mighty stream.
>
> *(5:21-24)*

At another time, Amos lashed out in a similar vein:

> Hear this, O ye that swallow up the needy,
>> even to make the poor of the land to fail. . . .
> The LORD has sworn by the excellency of Jacob:
> Surely I will never forget any of their works. . . .
> And I will turn your feasts into mourning,
>> and all your songs into lamentation;
> And I will bring up sackcloth upon all loins,
>> and baldness upon every head;
> And I will make it as the mourning of an only son,
>> and the end thereof as a bitter day.
>
> *(8:4, 7, 10)*

The prophecy of Amos is a treasure of spiritual insight and prophetic ardor. It is a beautiful example of God's unexpected ways, when a blunt, unschooled shepherd of Judah can stand before the mighty leaders of Israel and fulminate against their sins. Amos is a man after every Christian's heart. For there is a gospel in Amos, said George L. Robinson, but it is "the gospel of the Lion's Roar!"

ISAIAH

In several important ways, Isaiah is generally regarded to be the prince of prophets. To begin with, his prophecy is the first one we encounter in the Bible as it is arranged. Then, it is the longest of all prophetic books; in fact, it is second only to the Psalms among all Old Testament books. Isaiah is also known as the Evangelical Prophet because he said so much about the future ministry of the Messiah. Finally, Isaiah was well educated and literate, a man of high birth and wide prestige in Judah. Unlike Amos and his rural background, Isaiah was a product of the city, with influence even in the king's palace.

Isaiah, the son of a man named Amoz (not to be confused with Amos, the prophet to Israel), was a prophet in Judah for forty years during the reigns of Uzziah, Jotham, Ahaz, and Hezekiah. From his position as counselor to the king and citizen of Jerusalem, he saw the corruption of the nation at close hand. He saw the rising power of Assyria, which would soon take the Northern Kingdom away. He was born in momentous times and saw wickedness all his days, but, like most great men, he was equal to the challenge of his time.

Isaiah notes his call at the close of Uzziah's fifty-two year reign, during which the nation had greatly prospered. The prophet saw the state of corruption that had come with the prosperity, and spoke vigorously against it:

> Ah sinful nation,
> A people laden with iniquity,
> A seed of evildoers,
> Children that are corrupters:
> They have forsaken the Lord,

> They have provoked the Holy One of Israel unto
>   anger,
> They are gone away backward.
>
> *(1:4)*

Isaiah, like Amos, condemned the hypocricy of the people, who offered sacrifices with bloody hands:

> To what purpose is the multitude of your sacrifices
> unto me?
> saith the Lord:
> I am full of the burnt offerings of rams,
> and the fat of fed beasts;
> and I delight not
> in the blood of bullocks, or of lambs, or of he goats.
> Your new moons and your appointed feasts
> my soul hateth:
> they are a trouble unto me;
> I am weary to bear them.
> And when ye spread forth your hands,
> I will hide mine eyes from you;
> yea, when ye make many prayers,
> I will not hear: your hands are full of blood.
>
> *(1:11, 14, 15)*

Although Isaiah, like all Old Testament prophets, spoke against the evils of his day, his most important work related to the coming of the Messiah. In view of this, it is not surprising that he is quoted in the New Testament more than any other prophet. He is quoted by name twenty-one times, and is alluded to many others.

The statesman prophet foretold many things about Christ and His ministry, specifically, His virgin birth:

> Therefore the Lord himself shall give you a sign;
> Behold, a virgin shall conceive, and bear a son,
>   and shall call his name Immanuel.
>
> *(7:14)*

and His advent on earth:

> For unto us a child is born,
>   unto us a son is given:
>   and the government shall be upon his shoulder:
> and his name shall be called Wonderful, Counsellor,
>   The mighty God,
>   The everlasting Father, The Prince of Peace.
>   *(9:6)*

and His humanity, as the offspring of David:

> And there shall come forth a rod out of the stem of
>   Jesse,
>   and a Branch shall grow out of his roots:
> And the spirit of the Lord shall rest upon him,
>   the spirit of wisdom and understanding,
> the spirit of counsel and might,
>   the spirit of knowledge and of the fear of the
>   Lord.
>   *(11:1, 2)*

and the righteousness of His lordship upon the earth
(11:2-5).

The greatest of all Messianic prophecies, and the crowning section of what Isaiah has to say, is his prediction of the Lord's vicarious suffering:

> He is despised and rejected of men;
>   a man of sorrows, and acquainted with grief:
> and we hid as it were our faces from him;
>   he was despised, and we esteemed him not.
> Surely he hath borne our griefs,
>   and carried our sorrows:
> yet we did esteem him stricken,
>   smitten of God, and afflicted.
> But he was wounded for our transgressions,
>   he was bruised for our iniquities:
> the chastisement of our peace was upon him;
>   and with his stripes we are healed.
>   *(53:3-5)*

The full prophecy is an extended section, chapters
52:13-53:12. To this must be added the prophecies
that look beyond the first advent to the Millenium yet
to come (see chapters 2, 11, 12, 24-27 and 59-66).

Above all else, the Book of Isaiah amounts to a
beautiful expectation of Christ, the Savior and Lord.

MICAH

Contemporary with Isaiah was a prophet named
Micah, also a native of Judah, who preached to both
Israel and Judah. Although he and Isaiah lived at the
same time, Micah was more like Amos in background
and ministry. He was a native of Moresheth-gath, near
the Philistine border (1:14), and his message was a
single declaration against the sins of the two kingdoms.

Despite the personal differences between the two
men, there were striking similarities in the preaching
of Micah and Isaiah:

> And it shall come to pass in the last days,
> that the mountain of the Lord's house shall be
>   established in the top of the mountains,
>   and shall be exalted above the hills;
>   and all nations shall flow unto it.
>
> *(Isaiah 2:2)*

> But in the last days it shall come to pass,
> that the mountain of the house of the Lord shall be
>   established in the top of the mountains,
>   and it shall be exalted above the hills;
>   and people shall flow unto it.
>
> *(Micah 4:1)*

John Howard Raven, in *Old Testament Introduction*, has
found nineteen parallel passages in the two prophecies
of Isaiah and Micah, which is understandable in view

of the fact that the two men lived at the same time and preached about similar conditions.

Israel was prosperous and wicked, as was Judah, and Micah condemned the foundation of wickedness upon which the prosperity stood. Like Amos, he was particularly furious with the wealthy landlords who oppressed the peasantry of Israel:

> Woe to them that devise iniquity,
>   and work evil upon their beds!
> when the morning is light, they practise it,
>   because it is in the power of their hand.
> And they covet fields, and take them by violence;
>   and houses, and take them away:
> so they oppress a man and his house,
>   even a man and his heritage.
>
> *(2:1, 2)*

He used even more imaginative language against the princes of Israel,

> Who hate the good, and love the evil;
>   who pluck off their skin from off them,
>   and their flesh from off their bones;
> Who also eat the flesh of my people,
>   and flay their skin from off them;
> and they break their bones,
>   and chop them in pieces, as for the pot,
>   and as flesh within the caldron.
>
> *(3:2, 3)*

Many of the wealthy Israelites believed themselves to be righteous despite their greed and cruelty, because they offered sacrifices and observed Jewish ritual. Not so, said Micah forcefully:

> Will the Lord be pleased with thousands of rams,
>   or with ten thousands of rivers of oil?
> He hath shewed thee, O man, what is good;

and what doth the Lord require of thee,
    but to do justly,
    and to love mercy,
    and to walk humbly with thy God?

(6:7a, 8)

Micah was the last prophet to Israel before the kingdom fell to Assyria in 721 B.C., never to rise again. He lived to see that tragic end to the ten northern tribes. Even as the curtain was about to be drawn forever on faithless Israel, a ray of light was seen in more noble Judah to the south. Micah turned his attention to a small Judean town named Bethlehem, and said:

But thou, Bethlehem Ephratah,
    though thou be little among the thousands of
    Judah,
Yet out of thee shall he come forth unto me that is to
    be ruler in Israel;
whose goings forth have been from of old,
    from everlasting.

(5:2)

Israel, to whom Micah preached, might fall, but the Messiah of whom he preached would come forth as a ruler in Israel forever.

DISCUSSION QUESTIONS

1. What was the subject of the writing of Obadiah? Why was Edom a natural enemy of Judah?

2. Of what great natural calamity did Joel write, and what was his message to the people?

3. Why was Jonah so unwilling to preach to the city of Nineveh?

4. What message did Jonah preach to the people of Nineveh, and what were the results of his ministry?

5. Explain the two divisions of the Book of Hosea and what they contain. Why did God direct Hosea to marry an adulterous woman?

6. What was the burden of the message of Amos and to whom was it directed?

7. Isaiah is generally regarded to be the prince of the prophets. To what great event did many of his prophecies point?

8. Who was the last great prophet to Israel before the kingdom fell to Assyria?

Four   7
Contemporary
Prophets

In 722-721 B.C. the Northern Kingdom (Israel) was conquered by Assyria and most of its finest people were deported to Assyria. The Southern Kingdom (Judah) survived alone for 150 years. Four prophets arose in that period—Nahum, Zephaniah, Jeremiah and Habakkuk—to guide the surviving Jewish nation. The four prophets lived and preached during the same fifty year period, 650-600 B.C.

Judah, like Israel, stood in constant danger of being conquered and its people deported. Much of the nation's spiritual concern was aimed at preventing that from happening, for Judah was ringed by enemies eager to bring about its defeat.

NAHUM

The first prophet of record following the fall of Samaria (Israel) was Nahum, a citizen of Elkosh, which was probably the early name of Capernaum. Capernaum means "City of Nahum." The occasion of Nahum's prophecy was the impending downfall of Nineveh, capital of Assyria, the violent enemy of Israel. Assyria had recently conquered Israel, and now the judgment of God would fall on Nineveh.

The effect of Jonah's ministry to Nineveh had
ended and the great city was as wicked as ever, so
Nahum spoke of its impending doom. The short
prophecy (three chapters) consists of an opening chapter of praise to God:

> God is jealous, and the Lord revengeth;
>   the Lord revengeth, and is furious;
> the Lord will take vengeance on his adversaries,
>   and he reserveth wrath for his enemies.
>
> *(1:2)*

Following the majestic psalm of praise, there are two
chapters that speak of God's judgment of Nineveh. He
who had spared the city when it repented in the time
of Jonah, would not spare it again. Nahum's descriptions are vivid and powerful:

> But Nineveh is of old like a pool of water. . . .
> She is empty, and void, and waste:
>   and the heart melteth, and the knees smite
>   together,
> and much pain is in all loins,
>   and the faces of them all gather blackness.
>
> *(2:8, 10)*

The reason for the judgment on Nineveh is spelled
out bitterly:

> Woe to the bloody city!
>   it is all full of lies and robbery;
>   the prey departeth not;
> Because of the multitude of the whoredoms of the
>   wellfavored harlot,
>   the mistress of witchcrafts,
> that selleth nations through her whoredoms,
>   and families through her witchcrafts.
>
> *(3:1, 4)*

Nahum's book, totally poetic in form, is one of the most colorful, imaginative and vigorous of all the prophetic books. It is filled with talk of vengeance against Nineveh. Nineveh, and all Assyria, was an old and hated enemy of Israel (which is why Jonah objected when God spared it), and the hatred only deepened when Assyria destroyed and humiliated Israel. So Nahum has nothing but anticipation and joy at the thought of Nineveh's destruction. The prophet found divine vengeance a delightful prospect:

> Thy shepherds slumber, O king of Assyria:
>   Thy nobles shall dwell in the dust. . . .
> There is no healing of thy bruise;
>   Thy wound is grievous:
> All that hear the bruit of thee shall clap the
>   hands over thee:
>   For upon whom hath not thy wickedness passed
>   continually?
>
>   (3:18, 19)

ZEPHANIAH

Zephaniah, a contemporary of Nahum and Jeremiah who lived in Jerusalem during the reign of Josiah, is especially concerned with the approaching judgment upon Judah, whose sins equalled those of the Northern Kingdom before it fell. The prophet also foretells the judgment that will befall Philistia (Gaza), Moab, Ammon, Ethiopia and Assyria (2:4-15). The prophecy can be called apocalyptic, because it views the divine judgment that is to come upon the nations of the earth. Its main emphasis is upon the judgment of Jerusalem and Judea (3:1-7).

Zephaniah's descriptions of the day of wrath are as vivid as any in Scripture:

And it shall come to pass in that day, saith the Lord,
that there shall be the noise of a cry from the fish
        gate,
    and a howling from the second,
    and a great crashing from the hills.
                         (1:10)

The great day of the Lord is near,
    it is near, and hasteth greatly,
even the voice of the day of the Lord:
    the mighty man shall cry there bitterly.
That day is a day of wrath,
    a day of trouble and distress,
    a day of wasteness and desolation,
    a day of darkness and gloominess,
    a day of clouds and thick darkness.
                         (1:14, 15)

For my determination is to gather the nations,
    that I may assemble the kingdoms,
to pour out upon them mine indignation,
    even all my fierce anger;
For all the earth shall be devoured
    with the fire of my jealousy.
                         (3:8)

The sins of Jerusalem are many, but that which
most certainly brings down the wrath of God is the
faithlessness of the religious leaders. The vilest sin is
that which is found in men who claim to be good,
those with the responsibility for the spiritual well
being of others.

    Her princes within her are roaring lions;
    Her judges are evening wolves
    They gnaw not the bones till the morrow.
    Her prophets are light and treacherous persons:
    Her priests have polluted the sanctuary,
    They have done violence to the law.
                    (3:3, 4)

Zephaniah's prophecy, still in the vein of an apocalypse (a prophecy in which God destroys the ruling powers of evil and raises the righteous to life in a Messianic kingdom), foretells the preservation of a remnant of righteous souls in Israel who will enjoy the presence and blessings of God in Jerusalem:

> In that day it shall be said to Jerusalem:
> Fear them not:
> And to Zion,
>   Let not thine hands be slack.
> The Lord, thy God, in the midst of thee is mighty;
> He will save, he will rejoice over thee with joy,
> He will rest in his love,
> He will joy over thee with singing.
>
> *(3:16, 17)*

JEREMIAH

Jeremiah was one of those whom we call Major Prophets because of the length of his writings. He lived in Anathoth, a small town near Jerusalem, during the bleak days before Judah's overthrow by Babylon. It was a tragic time, and Jeremiah was born for the express purpose of preaching in it. God spoke thus to him, "Before I formed you in the womb I knew you, and before you were born I consecrated you; I appointed you a prophet to the nations" (1:5).

Jeremiah spoke much about his call to be a prophet (see 1:6-10; 20:9), probably because he lived in a time when there were many false prophets. He wanted to establish the validity of his work for God. Jeremiah preached for about fifty years, beginning at the age of twenty, when Josiah was king, and continuing until Jerusalem was destroyed during Zedekiah's reign. In the course of his long ministry, Jeremiah saw the gradual demise of his nation, the treachery of numerous false prophets who gave bad advice to the leaders, and Judah's frantic efforts to stay the hand of doom.

The written prophecy is in the form of sermons given during the fifty years of the prophet's activity. Jeremiah had a scribe named Baruch who "wrote upon a scroll at the distation of Jeremiah all the words of the Lord which he had spoken to him" (36:4, 6, 18, 27, 28, 32).

The Message of Jeremiah

Throughout his lifetime, Jeremiah was able to see the approaching doom of his nation. Judah would soon follow the fate of Israel by suffering defeat and deportation from their homeland. As Israel fell to the Assyrians, Judah would fall to Babylon. Jeremiah saw the approaching doom and urged the leaders to repent of their evil and seek peace with Babylon. But the leaders wanted no such advice; so they sought alliances with Assyria and Egypt in the belief that they could withstand Babylon.

> Have you not brought this upon yourself
>   by forsaking the LORD your God,
>   when he led you in the way?
> And now what do you gain by going to Egypt,
>   to drink the waters of the Nile?
> Or what do you gain by going to Assyria,
>   to drink the waters of the Euphrates?
> Your wickedness will chasten you,
>   and your apostasy will reprove you.
> Know and see that it is evil and bitter
>   for you to forsake the LORD your God;
>   the fear of me is not in you,
> says the Lord GOD of hosts.
>
> (2:17-19, Revised
> Standard Version)

Judah had many false prophets who said Jeremiah

was wrong. God had always come to the rescue of His
people and He would do so again.

> A wonderful and horrible thing
>   is committed in the land;
> The prophets prophesy falsely,
>   and the priests bear rule by their means;
> And my people love to have it so:
>   and what will ye do in the end thereof?
>
> *(5:30, 31)*

> They have healed also the hurt of the daughter of
>   my people lightly,
>   saying, Peace, peace,
>   when there is no peace.
>
> *(6:14)*

> Thus saith the Lord;
> Cursed be the man that trusteth in man,
>   and maketh flesh his arm,
>   and whose heart departeth from the Lord.
>
> *(17:5)*

A great deal of historical narrative is in Jeremiah,
which enables us to follow the decline of the nation,
who mistakenly believed their alliances with Egypt and
Assyria would secure them from Babylon. "Do not
listen to your prophets, your diviners, your dreamers,
your soothsayers, or your sorcerers, who are saying to
you, 'You shall not serve the king of Babylon.' For it is
a lie which they are prophecying to you, with the
result that you will be removed far from your land . . ."
(27:9, 10, *Revised Standard Version*).

Because of his rather doleful prophecy, Jeremiah
has been called "the weeping prophet"; and a long
speech of complaint or pessimism is called a *jeremiad*.

The truth is that Jeremiah spoke unpleasant truth
in a day that men wanted to be lulled with lies. His
word proved true when Nebuchadnezzar and the

Babylonians overwhelmed Judah and carried the choice men of Judah into Babylon. Chapter 52, the closing chapter, tells how Judah came to an end—and a horrible story it is. King Zedekiah had his eyes gouged out (52:11) and the Jews were taken captive into Babylon.

Jeremiah's distinguished ministry spanned the decline and fall of the Jewish nation. He witnessed the sad deportation of the Jews to Babylon, although he personally (by that time he was an old man) was allowed to remain in Judah (39:11, 12). The prophet later went to Egypt, where he spent the last years of his life (chapters 43, 44).

HABAKKUK

The fourth of the contemporary prophets in Judah was Habakkuk, of whom we know very little. From his notation in 3:19, "To the chief singer on my stringed instruments," it is deduced by many scholars that he was a member of the temple choir or a Levite.

He was a contemporary of Jeremiah and he also prophesied just before the Babylonian invasion, but his ministry was much shorter than Jeremiah's. Both men lived to see the destruction of their homeland and the deportation of their people.

The Book of Habakkuk consists of a dialogue between the prophet and the Lord: Habakkuk asks two questions, which the Lord answers. The first question was *why does evil triumph over righteousness?*

> Therefore the law is slacked,
>   and judgment doth never go forth:
> For the wicked doth compass about the righteous
>   therefore wrong judgment proceedeth.
>
> *(1:4)*

To this, God's reply was that the Babylonian (or Chaldean) invasion was punishment for Judah's sins (1:5-11).

Habakkuk's second question was *why would God punish wickedness with people even more wicked?*

> Thou art of purer eyes than to behold evil,
>> and canst not look on iniquity:
> Wherefore lookest thou upon them that deal
>> treacherously,
>> and holdest thy tongue when the wicked devoureth
>> the man that is more righteous than he?
>>> *(1:13)*

To which God replied that the Chaldeans themselves would be punished (2:2-20).

> Behold, his soul which is lifted upright in him:
>> but the just shall live by faith. . . .
> Woe to him that buildeth a town with blood,
>> and establisheth a city by iniquity! . . .
> For the earth shall be filled
>> with the knowledge of the glory of the LORD,
>> as the waters cover the sea.
>>> *(2:4, 12, 14)*

The brief book closes with a prayer psalm by Habakkuk, in which he acknowledges the defeat of Israel to be the judgment of God. Yet the prophet believes in and depends upon the mercy of God.

> Although the fig tree shall not blossom,
>> neither shall fruit be in the vines;
> the labour of the olive shall fail,
>> and the fields shall yield no meat;
> the flock shall be cut off from the fold,
>> and there shall be no herd in the stalls:
> Yet I will rejoice in the Lord,
>> I will joy in the God of my salvation.
>>> *(3:17, 18)*

DISCUSSION QUESTIONS

1. Name the four prophets who preached to the Southern Kingdom (Judah) after Israel was conquered by Assyria.

2. What is the theme and burden of the Book of Nahum?

3. According to Zephaniah what class of people is more certain to reap the wrath of God?

4. What was the underlying message of the prophecy of Jeremiah? How was his message received?

5. What two dramatic questions did Habakkuk ask God? Discuss the answers.

Prophets
in Exile

8

Among the choice young Jews taken by force from Judah to Babylon were two who would be spokesmen for God in the foreign land. It is not difficult to imagine the unhappy circumstances of their ministry, separated from their own nation, surviving amidst people, customs and laws all that were unfamiliar to them.

Daniel and Ezekiel had to be extraordinary men to do the work they did. But they were not alone. Living in the transplanted Jewish community were many men of equal valor and ability. In the Historical Books of the Bible we read of numerous exiles who were men of valor—prominent among whom were Daniel and Ezekiel.

DANIEL

Daniel and three friends were chosen from among those taken to Babylon to serve in the king's household. The historical account of the four favored young men takes up six of the book's twelve chapters. The religious pressure aimed at compelling the Hebrews to worship King Nebuchadnezzar resulted in two of the most famous miracles of the Bible. In the first, Daniel's friends—Shadrach, Meshach, and Abednego—were condemned to be burned in a furnace, but God delivered them from harm (3:1-30). In the second, during the reign of Darius, Daniel himself was cast into a den of lions, but God intervened and the lions did no harm to Daniel (6:12-23).

God did not prevent His servants from being consigned to the places of peril; He saved them in their peril. In similar fashion, God does not always spare us from trouble or danger—He preserves us in time of trouble. "So Daniel was taken up out of the den, and no manner of hurt was found upon him, because he believed in his God" (6:23).

An Apocalypse

Because of its lengthy historical sections, the Book of Daniel was classified as a Historical Book in the Hebrew canon. With its record of such worldly rulers as Nebuchadnezzar, Belshazzar and Darius; with accounts of Babylon, the Chaldeans, the Medes and Persians, in addition to the Hebrew record, the Book of Daniel can accurately be classified with the Historical Books.

But it is more. It is an apocalypse, a book of prophecy, foretelling situations that exist right down to our time. Chapters 7-12 consist of visions and dreams that extend the prophetic view forward to the time of the end. Merrill F. Unger, in *Introductory Guide to the Old Testament*, calls Daniel:

. . . one of the most important prophetic books of the Old Testament . . . an indispensible introduction to New Testament prophecy, the chief themes of which are the apostasy of the church, the revelation of the man of sin, the great tribulation, the second coming of Christ, the resurrections and the establishment of the millennial kingdom.

All of these are foretold in the visions of Daniel. This

fact makes Daniel one of the most popular, most analyzed, most written about, and most criticized books of Old Testament prophecy. It has had more books written about it than most in the Old Testament, principally because of its apocalyptic sections. (There are many excellent evangelical studies of the prophetic revelations of the book).

Daniel saw the resurrection of the dead as an event of brightness for those who serve God. His view of the great day is unsurpassed in an Old Testament book.

And many of them that sleep in the dust of the earth shall awake, some to everlasting life, and some to shame and everlasting contempt. And they that be wise shall shine as the brightness of the firmament; and they that turn many to righteousness, as the stars for ever and ever. But thou, O Daniel, shut up the words, and seal the book, even to the time of the end: many shall run to and fro, and knowledge shall be increased.

(12:2-4)

EZEKIEL

Ezekiel was the second exile in Babylon whom the Lord called to speak and write for Him. Like Daniel, he had been carried away captive to Babylon, where he lived in the Jewish colony in Telabib on the river Chebar. Ezekiel was a member of a priestly family, whose father was named Buzi (1:1-3). Because he lived in Jerusalem before he was deported, it is possible that he knew Jeremiah, and he almost certainly knew Daniel.

Ezekiel was a married man, whose beloved wife died in the Babylonian exile (24:15-18). As frequently was the case, the prophet's personal life is entwined with his prophecy. It is significant that God chose as His prophets men who shared the experiences of the people.

The stage for Ezekiel's prophecy is set in the plaintive "Psalm of the Exiles" (Psalm 137), where the exiles contemplated the tragedy that had befallen Jerusalem. The heavens had been silent as to why God had allowed the Babylonians to crush the Jews. Then, on the river Chebar, the answer came at last to Ezekiel: Jerusalem had been the victim of a spiritual conspiracy between the princes, priests, prophets and people (22:23-30).

"Therefore," said the Lord, "have I poured out mine indignation upon them; I have consumed them with the fire of my wrath: their own way have I recompensed upon their heads" (22:31). Much of Ezekiel's prophecy is contemplation of what happened to the Holy City and the land of Judah. Much is said about the hypocrisy in the land before the fall, especially among the religious leaders:

Son of man, thou dwellest in the midst of a rebellious house, which have eyes to see, and see not; they have ears to hear, and hear not. . . .

(12:2)

Son of man, prophesy against the prophets of Israel that prophesy, and say thou unto them that prophesy out of their own hearts, Hear ye the word of the Lord: Thus said the Lord GOD: Woe unto the foolish prophets, that follow their own spirit, and have seen nothing! . . .

(13:2, 3)

Then came certain of the elders of Israel unto me, and sat before me. And the word of the LORD came unto me, saying, Son of man, these men have set up their idols in their heart, and put the stumblingblock of their iniquity before their face: should I be inquired of at all by them? . . .

(14:1-3)

Son of man, prophesy against the shepherds of Israel,
prophesy, and say unto them, Thus saith the Lord God
unto the shepherds: Woe be to the shepherds of Israel that
feed themselves! should not the shepherds feed the flock?

(34:2, 3)

Mystical Passages

The prophecy of Ezekiel has many allegorical and
mystical sections that make the book difficult for some
to understand. For example:

> The Four Wheels, 1:15-21
> The Eagles and the Cedar, 17:1-6
> The Drawn Sword, 21:1-32
> The Boiling Pot, 24:3-14
> Valley of Dry Bones, 37:1-14

In addition to his allegories, Ezekiel, with the stamp
of a true prophet, frequently spoke beyond the persons he addressed to the authority behind them. A
clear example of this is when he spoke to the king of
Tyre (28:11-19), but obviously intended Satan himself.
Of no human could he have said such things as:

> Thou hast been in Eden the garden of God;
>   every precious stone was thy covering,
> the sardius, topaz, and the diamond,
>   the beryl, the onyx, and the jasper,
> the sapphire, the emerald, and the carbuncle,
>   and gold: the workmanship
>   of thy tabrets and of thy pipes was prepared in
>   thee
> in the day that thou wast created.
> Thou art the anointed cherub that covereth;
>   and I have set thee so;
> Thou wast upon the holy mountain of God;
>   thou hast walked up and down in the midst
>   of the stones of fire.

> Thou wast perfect in thy ways
>> from the day that thou wast created,
>> till iniquity was found in thee.
>>> *(28:13-15)*

It is significant that Ezekiel spoke so often of iniquity, which is sin among those who pretend to be righteous. He used the word *iniquity* or *iniquities* fifty-two times in his book. The prophecy is largely that—an examination of the sins of Israel that caused her downfall.

The prophecy of Ezekiel also predicts the coming judgment of the Palestinian neighbors of Israel: Ammon, Moab, Edom, Philistia, Tyre and Sidon, Egypt and Mount Seir.

It is also Ezekiel who tells of the last-days rise of Gog, in the land of Magog, that will precede the end of this age (38:1-39:16). Gog, the evil ruler of the north, will lead massive forces against Israel in a final effort to destroy the nation. The assault will fail and Israel will have a dramatic victory. But that is yet to come: the prophecy belongs to the future, along with the Revelation prophecies of Armageddon.

God used a lonely exile on the river Chebar in faraway Babylon to interpret much of what had happened to Israel and to tell much of what is yet to happen.

DISCUSSION QUESTIONS

1. What two outstanding prophets were spokesmen for God in the land of exile?

2. Why are the prophecies of Daniel of such major importance to us today?

3. Ezekiel deals especially with the iniquity of Israel. Explain the meaning of the word *iniquity* (used fifty-two times) and explain its significance in this setting.

Prophets
of the
Restoration

9

The Jewish exile in Babylon lasted for about seventy years. In 536 B.C. Cyrus, king of Persia, who conquered Babylon, permitted the Jews to return to their homeland and rebuild their temple in Jerusalem. The exiles returned home under the leadership of Ezra; shortly afterward, in 520 B.C., two prophets, Haggai and Zechariah, began to preach in Judah, with Haggai preceding Zechariah by two months. One final prophet, Malachi, also preached in Judah at a later time, and then, with him the written record came to an end.

HAGGAI

Haggai's ministry to Judah was a series of four discourses, given during a four-month period in 520 B.C. His work was a brief and simple encouragement to the Jews to rebuild the temple in Jerusalem. Fifteen years had passed since the exiles returned to Judah, and the people had long ago built homes for themselves. So Haggai asked:

Is it time for you, O ye, to dwell in your ceiled houses, and this house lie in waste?

(1:4)

121

Haggai's call to rebuild the temple had good results, and the temple was rebuilt without further delay (1:12-15). Those who had seen the earlier temple were struck by how inferior the new was to the old:

Who is left among you that saw this house in her first glory? and how do ye see it now? Is it not in your eyes in comparison of it as nothing?

(2:3)

Haggai gave four prophecies in the course of his ministry, as follows:
1. The call to rebuild the Temple, 1:1-15
2. The message of hope, 2:1-9
3. Purity and divine blessings, 2:10-19
4. To Zerubbabel, 2:20-23

Happily, he lived to see the fulfillment of his prophecies, a blessing not enjoyed by most of the prophets.

ZECHARIAH

Along with Haggai was the prophet Zechariah, the son of Berechiah and grandson of Iddo. Zechariah came from a priestly family and was very likely attached to the priesthood himself.

The prophecy has two main divisions:
1. Prophecies during the rebuilding of the Temple, chapters 1-8
2. Prophecies after the Temple was rebuilt, chapters 9-14

In the first section, Zechariah gave many symbolic discourses to drive home his point that God had indeed punished His people, but He had also watched over them during the seventy years' captivity, and He would be with them in Judah.

Therefore, thus saith the LORD: I am returned to
Jerusalem with mercies: my house shall be built in it, saith
the LORD of hosts, and a line shall be stretched upon
Jerusalem.

(1:16)

But now I will not be unto the residue of this people as
in the former days, saith the LORD of hosts. For the seed
shall be prosperous; the vine shall give her fruit, and the
ground shall give her increase, and the heavens shall give
their dew; and I will cause the remnant of this people to
possess all these things.

(8:11, 12)

The second section follows the poetic form in
prophesying the fall of Tyre, Sidon and Philistia and
the preservation of Jerusalem (9:1-10). Jerusalem would
be preserved for the coming of its king, whom they
had long awaited:

Rejoice greatly, O daughter of Zion!
   Shout, O daughter of Jerusalem!
Behold, the King cometh unto thee:
   He is just and having salvation;
lowly and riding upon an ass,
   and upon a colt the foal of an ass.

(9:9)

Zechariah prophesied that the king would be rejected
by his people, for which they will be chastened (11:4-14;
12:10-14). The coming of the Lord is seen, first in
battle against the nations arrayed against Jerusalem
(14:1-5) and then as king supreme over all the world
(14:5-9).

The prophecy of the final battle of God against the
ungodly nations is highly descriptive:

And this shall be the plague wherewith the Lord will smite
all the people that have fought against Jerusalem; Their

flesh shall consume away while they stand upon their feet,
and their eyes shall consume away in their holes, and their
tongue shall consume away in their mouth.

(14:12)

It is not difficult to imagine such a phenomenon in
this day of atomic destruction.

Zechariah closes with a glimpse of Millennial peace
(14:16-21), when worship and praise will be everywhere. The bells of the horses and the vessels of the
Lord's house shall all be sacred to the Lord: "Holiness
to the Lord" shall cover the land.

MALACHI

The last prophet to the returned exiles was Malachi.
Almost nothing is known about him except the book
that bears his name. It is believed that he lived after
Haggai and Zechariah, during the days of Nehemiah.
The Book of Malachi is the last book of the Old
Testament canon; it was followed by "four hundred
silent years" when no prophet of record appeared in
Israel.

Malachi wrote after the Temple had been rebuilt,
but the expected prosperity had not come. His prophecy is in two sections:

  1. The sins of Israel are reviewed, 1:1-2:17
  2. God's judgment on sinners, 3:1-4:6

The first section is an accounting of Israel's sin, much
like similar sections of other prophets. Sins between
husband and wife are specified (2:14), as was the
people's hypocricy (2:17) and their robbery of God by
deceit in tithing and giving (3:8-10).

The second section provides a forceful foretelling of
the Messiah.

Behold, I send my messenger, and he shall prepare
the way before me:
And the Lord, whom ye seek, shall suddenly come to
his temple,
Even the messenger of the covenant, whom ye delight
in:
Behold, he shall come,
saith the LORD of hosts.
But who may abide the day of his coming?
And who shall stand when he appeareth?

(3:1, 2)

But unto you that fear my name
Shall the sun of righteousness arise with healing in
his wings;
And ye shall go forth, and grow up as calves of the
stall.

(4:2)

The Messianic prophecy concludes with a promise
that God will "send you Elijah the prophet before the
coming of the great and dreadful day of the Lord"
(4:5). Four hundred years would pass before John the
Baptist fulfilled that prophecy. John would be called
"prophet of the Highest" (Luke 1:76), and Jesus
would say of him, "And if you will receive it, this is
Elias, which was for to come" (Matthew 11:14).

So the Old Testament closed, and the New Testament opened, with a prophet of the Lord.

DISCUSSION QUESTIONS

1. Name three outstanding prophets of the post-exilic period.

2. Haggai's work was to encourage Judah to rebuild the temple. Give four specific prophecies he gave during his ministry.

3. Explain the two main divisions of Zechariah's prophecy.

4. What aspects of Malachi's prophecy prepare the reader for the beginning of the New Testament period?

INSTRUCTIONS AND WRITTEN REVIEW
CTC 204—POETS AND PROPHETS OF ISRAEL

Instructions

1. A Certificate of Credit will be awarded when the student satisfies the requirements listed on page 7.

2. The student, at a time designated by the instructor, should prepare the written review following the guidelines listed below. The student should use blank sheets of paper and make his own outline for the review. The completed written review should be presented to the instructor for processing.

3. In the case of home study, the student should present his answers to the pastor or to someone the pastor designates.

Written Review

1. Name the six books of the Bible known as the Poetic Books. Why are they so called? To what do they owe their particular beauty?

2. Approximately what portion of the Scriptures was written in poetical form? In what poetic style is most of the poetry written?

3. The Psalms are arranged into five sections. Name some points which seem to characterize these divisions.

4. Explain the classification "narrative poetry" and tell which biblical books are narrative in nature.

5. What proof do we have that Job was an actual person who lived and not just an imaginary character?

6. By whom were the Proverbs written? Study the six natural divisions of the Book of Proverbs and identify the author of each.

7. Explain the differences in the two kinds of spiritual leaders in Israel: priests and prophets.

8. Of the sixteen prophets who wrote, four were called Major Prophets and twelve were called Minor Prophets. Name these and explain why they were so called.

9. Isaiah is generally regarded to be the prince of the prophets. To what great event did many of his prophecies point?

10. Who was the last great prophet to Israel before the kingdom fell to Assyria?

11. Name the four prophets who preached to the Southern Kingdom (Judah) after Israel was conquered by Assyria.

12. What two outstanding prophets were spokesmen for God in the land of exile?

13. Why are the prophecies of Daniel of such major importance to us today?

14. Name three outstanding prophets of the post-exilic period.

15. What aspects of Malachi's prophecy prepare the reader for the beginning of the New Testament period?